# CENTER
## of
# ATTENTION

## A TRUE CRIME MEMOIR

## Jami D. Brown Martin

Bella River Publishing
Laguna Beach, CA

Bella River Publishing/Center of Attention
Printed in the United States of America

Center of Attention/ Jami D. Brown Martin -- 1st ed.

ISBN 978-1-7362907-0-5 Print Edition

ISBN 978-1-7362907-2-9 Ebook Edition

*For my son, my reason for everything*

# A Note To Readers

CENTER OF ATTENTION represents a true account of my experiences as I remember them. While I have recreated some conversations based on my best memories of the information exchanged, sentiments expressed, and personalities involved, they're not intended to be exact records of what was said. As for the rest of the book, I understand that all memory is fallible—especially after several decades—perhaps all the more so when it comes to stressful events. I don't doubt that some who shared the experiences on these pages recall them differently. This memoir is not intended to dispute their recollections, only to offer my own honest account of my experience.

With respect to certain details of my family divorce history and the details of the crime, I relied on court documents, statements from mental health providers, police reports, and public accounts. Where I quoted documents and letters, the quotes are exact and based on material available to me.

I have changed certain names, conversations, and specific details of individuals in some instances to maintain anonymity and protect privacy as much as possible while maintaining a true and accurate account of my recollections. I have also changed some identifying characteristics and details such as physical properties, occupations, and places of residence. I strive to live a happy, healthy life and I want the same for my family, friends, and all the people who have been part of this story and my eventful existence.

# SCENE OF THE CRIME

I was making dinner and planning on a quiet evening home with my son when my phone rang and changed everything forever.

"Turn on the news!" said one of my many cousins with an edge I'd never heard in her voice. "Jason's all over the news!"

"Jason?" It had only been a few hours since my brother Jason left my house. We'd just spent a great week together. Had there been an accident? What was going on?

I picked up the remote and clicked on the TV.

*Jason Derek Brown... armed robbery... five shots, point blank range to the head...*

I changed the channel.

*Considered armed and dangerous...*

"Can't be," I managed to say, hanging up with my cousin and clicking to another station where my brother was again, impossibly, the lead story. All I could think was that there had to be some kind of huge mistake. My dad had gone missing ten years earlier, never to be heard from again. *Now Jason?* Already numb and in disbelief, I listened to multiple newscasters announce that my brother *my brother* was wanted in connection with the fatal shooting of Keith Palomares, a twenty-four year old Dunbar armored car driver, outside a movie theater in the Phoenix suburb of Ahwatukee. They

1

were saying he'd fled the scene on mountain bike with $56,000 in cash.

My landline and cell phone began to ring off the hook.

My teenaged son, Logan, was in the other room and he couldn't know what was going on. He'd already lost his dad and his grandfather. I turned off the television and silenced the phones.

Even the thought that Jason was being questioned in connection to something this awful was just too much.

Full of adrenaline, freaking out, and not knowing what else to do, I took two Xanax and poured myself the first glass from what would be an entire bottle of wine. As my panic and blood alcohol content rose exponentially, I grabbed my Jack Russell terrier's leash, clipped it on her, and tried to process what I'd heard.

As though that were possible.

One week earlier, on Tuesday, November 30, 2004, I was headed to the garage to get the boxes filled with lights and ornaments when my cell phone rang.

It was Jason.

"What are you doing?" he asked.

He knew me well enough to know I was getting out the holiday decorations. Every year, right after Thanksgiving weekend, I design my home for the holidays. As a child from a big Mormon family, Christmas was always a big deal—full of gifts and happy young memories. My dad would buy the biggest tree on the lot. Some years, it barely fit in our house. We had an elaborate, formal Christmas Eve at my grandparents' with all the aunts, uncles, and cousins. As kids, we ate on a dining table in the kitchen next to the maid's quarters and were waited on by the help until we were old enough to join the adults in the formal dining room. On Christmas morning, there were tons of presents under the tree—shiny bikes with banana seats, sporting equipment, and large boxes wrapped in pretty paper. Most years, it took all morning to unwrap all the presents.

It is one of the few traditions I look back on with true joy.

"Where are you? We miss you," I said. My son Logan adored his fun-loving uncle and we hadn't heard much from Jason in the past year.

"In Arizona," Jason said. "But I'm planning to visit you guys soon."

"Come any time!" I said. We'd had our problems as kids, but as adults we were very close and loved to hang out together. "We're around and would love to see you."

Jason was his usual upbeat, relaxed, but unpredictable self as we chatted for a few minutes about my recent move from Laguna Beach, California to nearby Rancho Santa Margarita. I'd moved because Logan had the opportunity to play varsity basketball for a private Catholic School that had the best team in Orange County. It was his junior year and neither of us were too thrilled about leaving Laguna but my ex, Logan's stepdad, insisted it was a crucial step for him to get recruited to a Division One basketball program at a good university.

At the end of the conversation, Jason promised he'd visit very soon. We hung up. As I headed out to the garage, my doorbell rang.

I turned to see who was there and spotted Jason on the front steps, grinning.

His black Escalade was parked in front of the house.

"Surprise!" he said.

I should have known. He loved surprising me. It wasn't the first time; growing up, our whole life was like a game. Given we were a family consisting of four athletic kids with tons of energy, it wasn't surprising that our mom sometimes grew exasperated by the nonsense. It was more like growing up with three brothers because the youngest, my sister, was a tomboy from the day she was born. We were always tickling or punching or pushing. We would hold someone down and tickle them until they were hurting, crying, or screaming for help. My dad would make us hold my brother, Jason, down and give him a pink belly.

My mom was always yelling, "Quit roughhousing!"

Our dad instigated the commotion and made everything a bet. When we were little, Dad would put a $100 bill on the table, recline in his La-Z-Boy, and say, "I will bet you..." Then, he'd flex his feet hard so we wouldn't be able to pull his shoe off. We'd get on both sides and we'd pull and pull. Suddenly, he'd point his foot and we'd go flying against the furniture. The harder we flew and landed, the louder he laughed.

As we got older, he would bet us twenty bucks we couldn't drink an entire jug of milk, or that we couldn't drink the juice from the hot pepper jar. Life was a game and there was money to win.

Thankfully, as adults, our jokes had taken the form of unexpected visits and gentler humor. I was delighted and excited to see my baby brother. We always had the best time together and I couldn't think of a more perfect way to kick off the holidays. I showed him to the guest bedroom and pointed out the closet for him to put his things away. When Jason showed up for a visit, he usually had an overnight bag and gifts for us. He always made sure we had everything we needed and was very generous. This time though, multiple duffels were piled into his SUV. The first bag Jason unpacked was filled with jacket, sweaters, cold weather clothing, gloves, and beanies. Another had warm weather clothing gear and a lot of bathing suits and shorts.

"So, you're moving in?" I joked as he proceeded to unpack what seemed like an endless amount of random stuff.

"You never know," he said with a laugh.

I honestly didn't care what he did or didn't bring with him. I was glad to see Jason, and even happier he planned to hang out for a while—hopefully until Christmas. Fun times were definitely ahead when we were together.

As soon as he finished unpacking, we headed off to a busy Italian restaurant for lunch, then went to pick up Logan from school. Logan was ecstatic. He and his Uncle Jason spent summers together for weeks on end, camping, fishing, boating, wakeboarding, and riding ATVs. Jason had all the toys, the cars, and the fun. Jason bought Logan his first dirt bike, his first electric scooter, basically his first of every toy. Logan idolized Jason. The fact that his larger-than-life uncle was also his buddy made life all that much more fun.

Logan often told me he wanted to be just like Uncle Jason.

He hated to leave with Jason around, but Logan was scheduled to spend the evening and the rest of the week with his stepdad. Although we'd split, James and I had open visitation with Logan. We had grown close as friends and had an amicable relationship, despite my having left him. Jason assured him they would do something when he came back that Sunday.

Logan left looking forward to it.

With my son gone, Jason and I were left to our own devices. We loved going out and having a good time and were long overdue for some well-needed "party time." We immediately decided it was time for a night on the town. When we went out together, we always turned heads and people often assumed we were boyfriend and girlfriend. We had lots of friends, made new ones easily, and loved being the life of the party. We could always get into any bar without waiting in line. Free drinks were sent our way and both of us left with business cards or phone numbers scratched on napkins—his with lipstick.

That first evening, we decided to go see a well-known local musician play at a venue down the street. We sat in the bar and ordered drinks. Jason always ordered a Captain and Coke. That was his drink, and he could certainly drink a lot of them. I remember Jason putting a large tip in the musician's jar. We drank, danced, and closed the place down.

We went out every night that week, making our way up and down the coast from Laguna to Newport Beach, hitting every local hot spot until two or three in the morning. Jason called a different group of friends, and we'd meet up with them at a restaurant or bar. I couldn't help but notice that he pulled aside his closest friend out of every group at some point in the evening for a private conversation.

"What'd you guys talk about?" I asked Jason more than once.

"Just catching up," he answered without elaborating.

Later, after I knew the truth, I asked his friends what Jason had said to them. One after another, they reported the same thing: *He just told me what a really good friend I was, how much he loved me, and how much he appreciated our friendship.*

In his way, he seemed to be saying "goodbye" for good.

Aside from the amount of clothing he'd brought along, and his need to connect with all of his friends, there were only a few other incidents that struck me as out of character for him.

"You need to slow the F… down," he said one evening as we were on our way out. "Why are you driving so fast?"

My siblings and I were all precise drivers, but we all had a need for speed. My dad had taught all of us to drive fast and we did just that. When Jason questioned me for driving exactly the way he drove, I thought it was a little weird, but not enough to question him about it. In retrospect, I also found it odd that Jason's taste in music had changed. We had always listened to the same kind of music, but now he was playing gangster rap with a lot of profanity.

On another evening, we stumbled in late and I didn't lock the front door.

"Do you know what happens to you when you don't lock the door?" he asked. All of the sudden he was shoving me into the Christmas tree we'd put up together. The tree fell over and decorations flew.

"Get off me," I said, shoving him back, although we were both laughing over the fallen tree. We still roughhoused as adults. "I'll lock the door, you freak."

"You need to," he said, and went to bed.

I took his weird behavior as drunken protectiveness.

That Sunday, we were both hung over, having a lazy day watching TV shows on the couch. Jason, who'd commandeered the remote, settled on a new reality show marathon about prison life in San Quentin.

"Why are you watching this crap?" I asked, as one episode bled into another.

"I'll never go somewhere like that," he kept saying. "I would never make it."

"Okay…" I said, half-wondering if he was still a little drunk from last night.

"Can you get me in to see your plastic surgeon this week?"

"For what?" I asked, now sure he was still buzzed.

"I was thinking I should get the scar above my eye fixed while I'm here," he said.

"I'll call tomorrow and see if I can get you an appointment," I said.

"Cool," he said. "Also, order me some Chinese food."

"Order your own Chinese food," I said tossing the cordless phone from the kitchen to the living room.

The phone hit him in the head.

"I'm so sorry," I said. "Are you okay?"

"I'm fine," he said, but kept rambling on about San Quentin.

I started getting the house in order as Logan was coming back home for the week. It was going to be a busy one because Jason was already making plans for their adventures.

The next morning, Monday, December 6, 2004, Jason drove Logan to school. From there, he said he had plans to meet our older brother, Brad, for a round of golf. I never really knew what they were up to, not unlike like my dad who would tell my mom he was headed to work, and then throw his golf clubs into the trunk of his car. If I ever asked my dad where he was going, he would give his standard reply to avoid further questions, "I am going to see a man about a horse."

"Dinner later?" I asked, Jason as he was leaving.

"Sounds great," Jason said.

That was the plan until he called later that afternoon.

"Is your house open?" he asked.

"Not right now. I'm running errands. What's going on?"

"The sprinkler went off inside my house in Arizona and it's flooded. I need to get my stuff and get back."

*Sprinkler system?* I remember wondering. I'd been to his house multiple times. It was older and spacious and I could picture the layout and the furniture, but I couldn't remember if there were sprinkler heads inside and thought it would be weird if there were.

"When are you going to be home?" he asked calmly.

"I'm on my way."

His black Escalade was parked in front of the house when I got there.

He gave me a thank you hug, which I found a little odd, but he seemed his normal self as he went into the bedroom and began to pack.

He took his sweet time, with no sense of urgency, folding and loading his belongings into the Escalade. When he was done, I walked him outside.

He gave me a big hug.

"When are you coming back?" I asked.

"I'll be back." He hugged me again, this time a little tighter and longer, then added, "Someday."

I'll never forget watching him drive off. I felt it in my gut—sickening and visceral. I hadn't experienced anything like that since the last time I saw my father, ten years earlier.

My father, John Brown, had trained us to always be on the lookout, to know who is around, to always check behind us to see if someone was following, and to be ready to run. To this day, if I walk by someone on the street, I can give you a full description down to the shoes he or she is wearing. On the evening of December 6, 2004, I was freaked out knowing the authorities were looking for my brother, so I didn't have to be all that observant to spot a car with government plates and a man sitting inside. It was clear I was being watched.

"Okay, just sit there, buddy," I said to myself as I walked by.

Then, I spotted another parked car with two people inside.

There was another around the corner.

My house was under surveillance.

I began to panic.

The police, or whoever they were, thought Jason was there. Were they going to confuse Logan for Jason? Without another thought, I went into full mama bear mode and sprinted back toward the house.

I made it to my front door and even managed to get my hand on the doorknob before I was jumped by multiple FBI agents.

"My son's in there! My son's in there!" I screamed, not letting go of the door. "You can't go in. My son can't know what's going on!"

The next few seconds were a dizzying, sickening blur of guns, vests, and the bleat of approaching helicopters. It took six agents to get me down on the ground because I had so much adrenaline and I was so worried about Logan.

They taped my hands behind my back and took me inside.

Just as I feared, they rushed Logan's room and pointed guns at him. I will never, ever forget the terror in my completely panicked fifteen-year-old son's eyes or the total horror I felt as they shouted, *GET ON THE GROUND!*

The FBI ripped my house apart, all the while yelling, "Where is your brother?"

Logan and I were scared to death and he clung to me until they separated us. I completely freaked out when they took each of us to different rooms and wouldn't let me talk to my son for hours. They proceeded to fire a million questions at me:

*What was he wearing?*

*How was he acting?*

*Where did he go?*

I answered their questions telling the FBI exactly what he had on and that he had multiple duffel bags filled with both warm and cold weather clothing. I stressed that he didn't seem to be in a hurry and was very calm, collected, and even mellow as he gathered his things and left. I certainly had no idea where he went beyond what he told me and said so. Repeatedly.

"When did he leave?" they asked.

I'd just spent every waking moment with Jason for a whole week. We hadn't left each other's side and he'd been relaxed and normal the whole time. If he'd really committed a crime, wouldn't he have fled the country from Arizona? Why did he come to my house and hang out with me? I knew Jason and what he was or wasn't capable of doing—at least I thought I did. I couldn't fathom that he was hanging out with me having murdered someone. I was overloaded with extreme anxiety, not to mention intoxicated from a bottle of wine and Xanax, and I was convinced there had to be some kind of mistake. Besides, I'd been long programmed—like my siblings—to do whatever needed to be done to protect each other. Especially when the police were involved. I worried that if the FBI found my brother, there was a great chance he'd end up dead.

Jason's voice echoed in my head. *I'll be back…someday.*

"Early afternoon," I heard myself answer. Jason had actually left around 4:00 PM, less than two hours earlier.

"What kind of car was he in?"

"A silver BMW M3 convertible," I said, even though he'd left in his black Escalade.

Because of me, they did an all-points bulletin for Jason stating he was in a silver BMW. Little did I know Jason's other car, a silver convertible BMW M3, had already been implicated in the crime itself.

The second the FBI left my house, I called Brad, who'd been with Jason that morning. Our brother Brad lived in the area, and although Jason had said he was headed to Brad's house after he dropped off Logan, I learned that they'd met in his office. Brad knew Jason was in trouble, because he'd received a call from the police in Arizona inquiring into Jason's whereabouts and had confronted him about it.

According to Brad, Jason played dumb.

After their meeting, Jason had apparently called me to meet him at the house and had then disappeared.

Crying, I told Brad what had transpired over the last few hours at my house, including everything I'd said to the FBI.

It was all just too much.

"Jami, you need to go tell the FBI exactly what really happened," he said. "You can't save Jason now. You've got to save yourself."

# BORN BAD

**M**y mom tells a story about stopping for McDonald's when Jason was nine. She had money to buy fries for everyone but herself. Jason noticed the kids were all eating, but she didn't have any.

"Why aren't you having anything?" he asked.

"I used all the money I had on you guys," she said.

He insisted on sharing his fries with her.

My baby brother Jason was a loving kid who got his feelings hurt easily. Practically every family photo we ever took of the six of us, the perfect Mormon clan complete with matching outfits, shows him with tear-streaked cheeks. The photo session would usually start off with Mom or Dad telling him to smile, he'd make a weird face, and then Brad, Carrie, and I would take turns picking on him until the tears came.

At the time, we lived at 1707 Malcolm Avenue in West Los Angeles and attended the Westwood Ward of the Mormon church along with our many cousins. My grandfather, Bernard Brown, was a prominent bishop. On the way home each week, Dad would let one of the kids sit in his lap and pretend to let us drive home.

The Osmond Family was also in our ward, so, once in a while, they would be in town and we would get to see Donny or Marie. This was the seventies when they had their own show and the arrival of the Osmonds meant a mob of groupies outside and inside the church. We felt like celebrities having them as part of our community. The church and its teachings were a huge part of our lives.

My mom told me that one morning she dropped Jason and Carrie off at Sunday school and Carrie began to cry.

Jason went over, sat next to her, and tried to console her. In the process, he began to cry too because he was so upset for our sister. That's just how Jason was. Unfortunately, there was another, much less endearing, side to my little brother. Jason was extremely lazy as a child. He didn't want to do his homework or anything that involved the word *work*. If my mom would ask him to grab something, or do something for her, he did his best to weasel out of it. Whatever it was he'd been asked to do often got reassigned to one of rest of us, especially me. Jason was determined to take the easy way out of everything.

In addition, Jason didn't have a lot of friends. He wasn't needy that way. He hung out with a couple of the boys who lived on our street but was mostly content to play with Carrie and do stuff with Brad. Jason did have a church friend and would play at his house all the time. That was until he stole the boy's silver dollar and spent it at the Little League snack bar.

A couple of days later, Jason was baptized and forgiven of all sin in the eyes of the church.

The boy, however, didn't want to play with him anymore.

Jason's fascination with lifting things that didn't belong to him started at a young age. Jason loved candy and we lived right near a 7-Eleven on Westwood Boulevard. It wasn't that he couldn't pay for treats, but he seemed to like the thrill of getting away with it.

"Where'd you get that candy?" my mother asked, the first time she caught him.

He lied, but she knew the truth.

When my father came home, Dad took Jason back to the store and made him return it. Dad was always the coach for any sport so he could control when my siblings played and what position they played. He was the cub master, the proud father in the audience at school events, and always there to show support. He cared. He hugged us, told us that he loved us, but he was also strict and scary. There was no talking back or arguing with him. Punishments were by the dreaded black belt which he pulled, loop by loop, from his pants.

In those days, a beating with the belt was an acceptable form of discipline. If we did something wrong, he would make us pull our pants down, and whip our bare butts. I would protect my bottom with my hands and suffered welts to my knuckles as well.

My father whipped Jason for stealing that day.

Jason always seems to get it the worst out of the four children. I think my dad was trying to beat the bad out of him. I remember trying to pull my Dad's large, stocky frame off of Jason when I couldn't take the screaming and crying. Often it would land me across the room, against a dresser or nightstand from the back-handed slap. If I'd just had the shit knocked out of me, or I'd just gotten smothered with a pillow, I got up, dusted myself off, and went to school the next day telling myself that everything was okay. My dad gave me hugs and I knew he loved me. It was just the way it was.

My brothers and sister grew angrier and angrier as they grew older.

Especially Jason.

# Coming Clean

The morning after my brother disappeared, I got out of bed super hungover and terrified. I hadn't slept at all. I had to call the FBI and correct my story. First, I called my ex-boyfriend and long-time friend and protector, Antonio. As soon as I told him what was going on, he insisted he be there as a witness and in case he needed to call an attorney for me. I was grateful because I was mortified I'd be led away in handcuffs.

My hands trembled as I dialed FBI Special Agent Lance Leising, who was in charge of the investigation. When he answered I said, "I need to tell you something…"

Antonio, who owned a large, successful company, arranged for us to meet in the conference room at his office. Within an hour, Lance Leising and most of the other agents who had taken part in the interrogation at my house the night before, showed up at Antonio's office.

"Do you remember me?" a detective whom I hadn't seen the day before asked.

I was in such agony and shock, I could barely recognize my own face, much less anyone else's.

"I was on your dad's missing persons case. When I saw Jason on the news I had to come and see what's going on here," he said.

19

Ten years earlier, my father had also gone missing, never to be found.

"This is crazy," the detective said.

"Insane," I barely managed.

Everyone filed into to the conference room.

"What more do you have to tell us?" Special Agent Leising asked, even before everyone was seated.

I took a deep breath and tried to calm myself by focusing on the warm, bright sunshine flooding the room. "I lied."

"I see," Leising said. "About?"

"I was drinking last night. I was in shock, and I didn't tell you the truth." I looked up and forced myself to meet Leising's gaze. "I told you my brother left in a silver BMW."

"He didn't?"

"He was in his other car," I admitted. "The black Escalade."

They all began to yell at me at once: *Are you kidding? You've interfered with a federal investigation... We could have caught him... This is obstruction of justice...*

I was done.

Screwed.

I'd told the truth and now my life was over.

I began to sob.

"I took Xanax and I drank a bottle of wine. I was scared to death," I finally choked out. "I was terrified for myself and my son, I had just been told my brother had murdered somebody, and I was out of my mind..."

No one said anything.

"...What if someone showed up at your front door and told you your wife had killed somebody? Wouldn't your initial reaction be to protect her?"

Eventually, one of the investigators broke the horrible silence. "We see this all the time. It's a natural reaction for a family member to protect their own."

There was conversation all around me, but none directed to me. A few minutes later, I heard one FBI agent whisper to another, "She is looking at obstruction of justice charges."

Then, I heard another one say, "She'll never survive in prison."

Did he want me to hear him say that? Was he trying to scare me?

Special Agent Liesing finally quieted the room. "Do you have any other information you want to give us at this time?"

I knew I had to tell them everything or I was done for. I managed to nod. "Jason didn't leave in the afternoon. He actually left a few hours before you arrived at my house."

Liesing exhaled deeply. "You need to tell your story again, every word of it, from beginning to end, without leaving anything out. Not one single word."

"Everything better check out this time," someone else added.

I collected myself and repeated exactly what happened. I was very careful and spoke slowly, pausing only to catch my breath or wipe my eyes while they recorded everything.

When I was done, Antonio asked, "Does she need an attorney?"

Glances were exchanged around the room.

"Not yet," Liesing finally said. "But she very well might."

I'd been in complete and utter shock since the FBI appeared at my house, but after the second round of questioning, my mind was in a million pieces. I knew Brad had tipped Jason off about what he'd seen on the news, but I didn't know how the FBI knew where I was or that Jason had been with me. I'd just moved to Rancho Santa Margarita and I was only going to stay there for a year. It wasn't like I was living in a place where everybody knew me.

"How did you know Jason was at my house?" I asked.

One of the FBI agents leaned over and said, "A family member called us."

"A family member called you and told you Jason was at my house?"

The man nodded.

"So you mean to tell me if this family member hadn't called, you would have never come to my house, terrified me and traumatized my son? As in, you would have given me a phone call during the week when my son was at school and we could have avoided this drama?"

"Yeah," was all he said.

As soon as I got home that day, I called every relative I could think of—and I have a bunch—multiple aunts, uncles, and at least twenty-nine first cousins. My eighth phone call was to a cousin in Laguna Beach.

Her husband had called me late the night Jason's story hit the news and said, "Hey, Jami, we want to mail you a Christmas card and we need your address."

I gave it to him.

"Do you know anything about someone calling the FBI and telling them Jason was at my house?" I asked his wife, my first cousin.

"I did," she said quietly.

"You did what? I just helped you with design work on your house. What do you mean you called the FBI on my brother?"

There was a long pause and she quietly whispered, "It was the right thing to do."

"Logan could have been shot and he's a complete mess. So am I. Why would you do something like that? How could you? We're family."

"I had to do what needed to be done," she said.

"I don't ever want to speak to you again," I said along with a few other choice words, and hung up on her.

I was furious at her for allowing us to be ambushed by the FBI, and for the lifelong trauma she'd caused both Logan and me. Although I recognized that if Jason had committed this terrible crime, this was really on him, but I still didn't even know for sure if my brother really was guilty. What if he was somehow falsely accused and was hiding somewhere cold, hungry, and alone?

What would I do if Jason showed up again?

Even though my brother was a wanted man, I feared I wouldn't say no if he reached out to me and needed help. I had no choice but make sure that wouldn't happen, so I disconnected my home phone and had my cell number changed.

My life had already been changed forever.

# The Sins of the Father

"Families are forever" is an often-heard phrase amongst Mormons. Mormons believe the family unit is intended to last *through Heavenly Father's plan* into eternity. Therefore, when someone in a family strays from the path of righteousness, everything possible must be done to help them. In the meantime, it's equally important to keep up outward appearances because families are everything.

Growing up, people would always say, *Oh, you're a Brown kid,* with a sense of admiration. From the outside, I'm sure it looked that way. We were an attractive, athletic, church-going clan of brothers, sisters, and cousins who lived on the same street. Of course, looks and images can be very deceiving.

Appearances were especially important to my grandparents, Bernard and Genevieve Brown. Bernie Brown owned and ran a successful insurance brokerage. Bernie also owned apartment complexes, real estate, and dealt in cars. He had his hand in a lot of things, so everyone admired the Brown family, and certainly their money. Bernie was very involved in the church and served as a bishop. Gen was a doting mom to their five children, the middle being my father, John. In 1971, Gen was one of four nationwide recipients nationwide of the LDS Mother of the Year award.

Bernard and Genevieve spent the earlier years building the insurance brokerage out of their home on Cashmere in Los Angeles. Gen worked tirelessly side by side with Bernie in their large office set up down by the garages. One day, a man announcing himself as a city inspector showed up to say the office was in a "strictly residential section" and in violation of city zoning laws. He also mentioned that the various cars my grandfather was always buying and selling were utilizing too much of the available parking on the street. Bernie apologized and ignored the warning.

When the man returned, Bernie assured him he was wrapping things up and would be moved into new office space by the end of the day. My grandfather was apparently so convincing that the inspector agreed to close the file. The city inspector did come back and tried to look through the windows, but Bernie had instructed Gen to keep the blinds closed at all times and not answer the door. This all too familiar theme of hiding from the authorities would recur over and over in my life with my own father.

So would the general dishonesty.

A business associate of Grandfather's, as we were raised to call him, once said, "Bernie Brown was one of the biggest crooks in Los Angeles."

In a letter from my great-grandmother (Gen's mother) to my dad she reported, "There seems to be a lot of uneasiness around the Cashmere house. I do not know the causes. Apparently, Bernie owing money to others is nothing to get disturbed about, yet where it's due them, the shoe is on the other foot. I think Gen is gradually awakening to this fact and she is showing signs of much worry, but she won't talk about it."

Another letter to my dad from my great-grandmother said, "John, your dad is full of sly confidence and tricks. Ever since I have known him from the very first, he has been hard to understand. He seems to be always cooking up a new experience and these new experiences are not usually *according to Hoyle* or on the up and up."

When I looked up the meaning, I learned that Sir Fred Hoyle was the final authority when disputes arose during card games in the 17th century. *According to Hoyle* literally meant, *In accord with the highest authority; in accord with a strict set of rules.*

My great-grandmother went on to say, "It's their life to do as they wish, but it hurts to stand by and see the inequities without saying a word. For the sake of my nerves and responsibilities, I prefer peace of mind and sanity."

Apparently, Grandfather's dishonest streak was not entirely surprising. Bernie's father, my great-grandfather, was a dentist in Los Angeles and word got around that he was a womanizer.

The lying and narcissism seemed to run in the genes.

Bernie eventually moved the insurance brokerage but still stayed at least ten more years in the downstairs office before it grew too large. He finally relocated to office space on Wilshire Boulevard in Westwood, and, later, to San Juan Capistrano on a big piece of land with a pond.

Along with the real estate Bernie owned, he also fixed, flipped, and raced cars. He passed his automobile infatuation down to my dad, and on to Jason. His financial success enabled him to bankroll a lot of the secret family drama that would unfold, much of it involving my dad.

Of their five children, Edward, the oldest, was something of the golden child. He was the picture-perfect successful son who grew up to become a tax attorney. I always liked my Uncle Edward who seemed nothing like Grandfather or my dad. He and his wife, who escaped Grandfather's stronghold on the rest of the family by moving to northern California, were both devoted Mormons. They raised seven children together. Edward also took in their niece and one of their son's friends from school. Uncle Edward and Karen loved helping others and their house was always a revolving door of kids who had lost their way and needed a family.

My dad also had an older sister Sherri who married and had five children. She was a wonderful mother, an amazing cook, and she loved to shop—a Brown gene I likely inherited. Tragedy struck again when undiagnosed cancer took her life, leaving her husband to father the children.

I never met my Aunt Laura who was apparently the 'wild' rebellious one. As a middle schooler, she wrote a letter to my dad, telling him that she had no one to talk to, saying, "Edward and Sherri are too perfect." She asked my dad about sex and told him she almost went *all the way*. She also said, "Sherri found beer cans in my bedroom and told on me."

Grandfather and Grandmother sent her off early to her freshman year of college to get her away from a boy. Laura was killed at age eighteen as a passenger in a car accident on her way back home for surprise visit from BYU. The driver, who was her friend and the sister of the boyfriend Laura had left to go school, survived the crash. Grandmother and Grandfather, who had warned her not to drive in bad weather during the winter months, were devastated.

Brooke, the youngest, married, had four kids, worked for Grandfather at the insurance agency, and hung close to the rest of the family.

When I was sixteen, Aunt Brooke said to me, "I'm not worried about you making it in life, Jami, because you've always known the difference between right and wrong."

"I definitely know what not to do in my life," I said. "John Brown has taught me everything that was illegal and wrong."

My dad, John, the middle child was definitely born "bad." He had problems with the law at a young age and grew up to be a con artist and a crook. He was scary, dark, and harmed other people physically, psychologically, and financially. At the same time, he could also be a loving caring father who would do anything for us and others. That's how sociopaths draw people in, with their charm and their willingness to always help. Sociopaths have little regard for the laws of society or other people and my dad was a textbook case. From everything I can tell, my father was not only predisposed to his behavior, but relished getting into trouble. People chose a side and they either loved or hated John Brown.

One night, at Sunday dinner with the extended family when my dad was five years old, seven-year-old Sherri wanted to give the blessing. At the end she added, "Please bless Johnny and help him do the right thing."

Even his older sister knew early on that little Johnny was mischievous and headed down a dark road.

As a young boy, my dad lived in his older brother Edward's shadow. While I believe my dad was born with a sociopathic streak, he may also have figured if he couldn't be the "good son" he was going to be the "bad son" to get attention. That is exactly what John Brown did. Athletic and handsome, John attended University High School on the west side of Los Angeles from 1957-1960. He played on the varsity football team during freshman, sophomore, and junior year. He was All-District and All-Conference. However, something "happened" at Uni High and John transferred to Beverly Hills High School for his senior year. Grandfather supposedly wanted John to graduate from a better-known school, so he rented an apartment in the school district and gave that as an address for John to enroll. That story doesn't make sense, because the transfer made him ineligible to play football senior year, which kept him from being widely scouted and offered scholarships at other colleges. At BHHS, he did wrestle later senior year, and came in third in the state championship in his weight class. He also lettered in baseball.

In June 1961, John graduated from high school. Even though he didn't play football his senior year of high school, he was accepted at Brigham Young University and headed off the summer after graduation to practice and play on the BYU Freshman football team.

In October, he was set up on a blind date with a pretty blond freshman from Texas named Jane. They dated a few more times. While Jane went to a couple of freshman football games and watched John play, she didn't fall for him, exactly.

By winter of 1962, just into his second semester of college, John was sent home from BYU for dishonesty and theft after filling a bag in a drugstore and walking out, a habit which would continue throughout his life.

That spring, John was called to a mission in Ireland. Young Mormon men are expected to dedicate two years to serve a mission to bring people to Jesus Christ and learn of his love for them. It was a controlled and disciplined environment for my unruly dad. Missionaries always have a "companion" by their side 24/7. Since they are not allowed to leave each other's side, he was carefully monitored. Did the rules and restrictions keep him in line? Little is known about what he really did on his mission. Most narcissists don't have a spiritual side, it is all for show to convince everyone that they are a good person. I do know that he loved his mission president, Stephen R. Covey (the proclaimed author of best-selling book: *The 7 Habits of Highly Effective People*). I also know his mission didn't make his weaknesses any stronger, because as soon as he returned, he was back to his old tricks. In fact, he brought home five emerald and gold rings from his mission, which he later gave to my mom.

My mom said she instantly thought, "Who did you steal these from?"

When he returned in 1964, John was given another chance at BYU because my grandfather had influence at the school and John agreed to get psychiatric care. Of course, he never attended his mandatory counseling sessions. He did, however, immediately start stalking my mom. For a budding narcissist like my dad, Jane was perfect—quiet, soft-spoken, naïve, not to mention beautiful. She was the ideal woman with whom he would have children and create an idyllic family front to hide behind while he lived his double life.

My mom didn't particularly want to date John Brown, but he would not leave her alone. Wide-eyed and easily misled, she had never experienced anything like him. John showered her with gifts. He seduced her with kindness. His persistence, the misimpression that he was great guy, and his ability to convince her that she was the most special beautiful person in the world soon prevailed. This is known as "love bombing," an effective tool in the narcissist toolbox. My mother was a simple girl. She'd worked from the time she was fifteen at an answering service after school and full time in the summer until she left for college. She'd worked after her first year of college for a year at the telephone company as a service representative to earn money to go back to school. She wasn't impressed by money, but she liked that he came from a big, respected Mormon family. When he sealed the deal by asking her to marry him, she said yes.

That Christmas, they traveled to Texas to meet my maternal grandmother.

My naïve, trusting mother had little idea what she was getting into. By early 1965, my dad had been sent home from BYU again for stealing. He convinced Jane he wasn't in the wrong, and nothing would ever happen like that again. He was a good Mormon who'd served his mission, was engaged, and was moving toward the kind of life expected of him as a respected member of the LDS church.

In order to marry within the walls of the temple, John and Jane had to get temple recommends and submit to worthiness interviews by church leaders. They had to keep holy ideals, which forbade everything from coffee, to profanity, to premarital sex. They wore the temple garments—special white underwear that consists of long shorts and a cap-sleeved shirt which covers the body from shoulders to thighs.

On April 24, 1965, Jane and John were married in the Los Angeles Temple and were "sealed" for eternity. The wedding was paid for by Grandfather and included a big shindig attended by all of their Los Angeles friends.

For their first year of marriage, my parents lived in a small efficiency house on Sepulveda boulevard owned by Grandfather. It had one room, a little kitchen, and a bathroom. At the end of the year, my parents moved to Texas so Jane could be close to her mother. She gave Jane the family house as a gift. They lived there for three years, paying $116 per month on the balance of the mortgage. My mom finished up her coursework at night, taking the credits she needed to return to BYU and graduate. John never went back to school, but took a job at Allstate Insurance, which was located inside a Sears store.

Within six months however, he'd been fired for theft—likely for stealing tools.

In 1965, my dad got a draft notice but wasn't drafted because they had a baby on the way. In the LDS church, one can only reach the "celestial kingdom" (the highest level of heaven) as a member of a family. Parents are taught to raise their children, "in love and righteousness, to provide for their physical and spiritual needs, to teach them to love and serve one another, to observe the commandments of God, and to be law abiding citizens wherever they live." Needless to say, they were both thrilled when my oldest brother Brad was born in the summer of 1966.

Within weeks of his birth though, five detectives appeared at the house with a warrant. Mortified, Mom held baby Brad in her arms and watched them search for items my father had stolen from another store. John was arrested for theft of a gun, postage stamps, and cookware. Mom had been taught that few things were more tragic than the implosion of the family. She'd planned on a life where Mondays would be devoted to "family night" and that daily prayer, devotion, and unity would keep the outside world's temptations at bay. This was not at all what she had in mind.

After a blip in the local newspaper about him being arrested, two counselors in the bishopric came to their house to talk to him about the incident. Mom felt she had no choice but move forward. She took her first job teaching PE and health in middle school. She became pregnant again in 1967 as she finished her first year of teaching and I was born in January of 1968.

Soon after, Dad told my mom that Grandfather had asked him to come back to California to be part of his insurance business. He also said he didn't want to raise his children in Texas because he considered the people to be less affluent and smart. Mom would later find out that Dad asked Grandfather if he could come back to California because he had blown it so bad in Texas with "stealing again."

We moved back to Los Angeles in 1968 when my brother, Brad, was not yet two and I was five months old. My dad's antics had been troubling but my mom had no idea how out of control he would become. Or that there'd be two more children to bind her that much more tightly to my father: Jason in July 1969, and Carrie two years later in the summer of 1971.

# CITY OF ANGELS
## 1968–1979

When they first arrived in Los Angeles, Grandfather told John and Jane there was a house across from Sherri and Bob that was a good investment. The price was $39,000. In those days you could have a house in Texas with a big circular drive for $50,000 so my mom was embarrassed to tell anyone back home that the well-worn, small house cost as much as it did. Jane never had a choice in the matter though—Grandfather bought the place with a down payment using his credit and she was told they would pay him back with the proceeds from the sale of the house in Texas.

On October 3, 1968, John Brown penned the following fake IOU to show Bernie he was making payments on the Malcolm house so it looked like my Mom and Dad did not own it:

*I do hereby agree to pay to Bernard W. Brown or Genevieve M. Brown 16,398.96 on or before Dec 31, 1975.*

*I appreciate Dad loaning us the money to buy the home, at 1707 Malcolm Avenue, and agree to pay him back soon as I am able to do so.*

Despite any objections on my mom's part, they unloaded the contents of a Ryder truck into their new house a few days later.

For the next eleven years, they would live on Malcolm Avenue in West Los Angeles with a $130 a month mortgage. The house was definitely convenient as it was right off Westwood Boulevard and down the street from the Los Angeles Mormon Temple. There's a Mormon church right behind the L.A. Temple called the Westwood Ward, which was in walking distance, and where we all attended and were part of the community.

From the outside, the Brown clan was the picture-perfect Mormon family. My fair-haired, petite, beautiful mom and dashing dad were the parents of two boys and two girls, all blond, blue-eyed, and athletic. From all outward appearances, we led blessed, busy, lives. Mom made sure of that, dressing us beautifully, keeping the house and yard tidy, and being involved in every aspect of our lives. She was on the PTA, a Brownie and Girl Scout leader, and drove my cousins, friends, and me down to Torrance three times per week for The Songsmiths, our singing and dancing group.

Bigger was always better in our family. We had a nice home, a motorhome, and a black limousine with a golden B embossed on the sides. Grandfather had the same model in silver. While the limo was admittedly a little odd, and people would stare whenever we pulled up anywhere, I have fond memories of my beautiful mommy driving the Brownie troop around or Dad taking us on road trips with the partition raised to separate the kid noise from my parents up front. While I was sometimes embarrassed to be dropped off in the limo at Bonner Private School in Brentwood, I loved that I got to go to the same elementary school wearing a matching uniform with my cousin.

Once, my mom was driving my cousin and me in the limo. She stopped at an intersection on Wilshire Boulevard. While she waited for the light to turn green, a homeless man thought we were offering him a ride so he opened the door and climbed into the backseat.

"There's a strange man back here!" I screamed. "Get him out of the car!"

Because the partition was up, it took what felt like forever before my mom heard me and realized what was happening. She pulled over and shooed the man out of the car without incident. It was traumatizing to be sure, but the symbolism of harboring a bum out for a joyride behind the darkened windows of the Brown family limo couldn't have been more apropos.

Nothing in our world was anything like it appeared...

Carrie was a Brownie, I became a Girl Scout, my brothers played Little League and were working to become Eagle Scouts, and mom and dad played den leader and cub master. We always felt like we had so much in terms of material possessions—the latest toys and sports equipment, the expensive Chemin de Fer jeans with rainbows on the butt I had to have— but life on Malcolm Avenue was anything but easy.

Within six months of moving back to Los Angeles, Grandfather fired my dad from his job at the insurance agency. From then on, Dad sold cars—fixing them up for people and making a little profit on each deal. My dad loved cars and the status they gave him. He practically lived at the auction where he would pick up new ones to resell for a few thousand here or there. We had cars constantly appearing in our driveway or in front of the house. Sometimes they were cool and fancy like Farrah Fawcett's dark green Corvette, and sometimes they were embarrassing junkers. When someone wanted to get rid of a vehicle, he'd offer to sell it for them. He used the church to find customers because a lot of people were trusting and he could use his family name for legitimacy.

The one thing every car he sold had in common was that he never hesitated to drive any of them, accumulating miles while he was supposedly looking for a buyer. That was, until repeated check-ins from the seller who inevitably showed up angry and demanded the car back.

He would talk people out of their anger by saying, "I just need another couple of weeks," and continue to drive the car. If he didn't sell it, he would turn back the odometer before he returned it to the unsuspecting seller. In the '70s, there was no way to find out the history of a car, when it was sold, or what the mileage was, so, with no security cameras and no computerized odometers, you could get away with a lot.

And he did.

The Department of Motor Vehicles was in frequent contact throughout this time because of complaints from victims, but also due to the fact that he would sell a car and not pay to transfer the title. A year after a sale, someone would get a ticket in the vehicle and discover that none of the proper paperwork was filed. He always came up with some kind of fake story to explain it off, but the truth was he hadn't followed through because he didn't want to pay the $100 fee to the state.

In addition to his automotive hijinks, my dad also engaged in a variety of other illicit activities. He gambled, often on the golf course. He stole, "whatever wasn't tied down," and began to submit false insurance claims to get funds from insurance companies. He'd walk out in front of a car and let it hit him, or slip at somebody's work, fake an injury, go to doctors and chiropractors, and file a claim with insurance. More than once, he was able to collect large sums. At one point, my mom went down to ninety-eight pounds because of an ulcerated esophagus. Dad took her to the doctor and made her use an assumed name so it wouldn't go on her health record and he wouldn't have to pay the bills.

My dad ruined his credit early on, so he used our names to get whatever it was he needed. He would also go get lines of credit at the casinos and then owe them money. The constant stream of illegal behaviors was an integral part of my dad's mentality. Crazy items would just appear in the house—everything from kitchen appliances to a fur coat. It was as though he woke up thinking about how he was going to con somebody or what he was going to steal that day.

"Where did this come from?" one of us would ask.

Dad would mumble some sort of lie. He never told any of us where the money for the elaborate gifts he would bring home at holiday time came from or what he was up to when he wasn't home.

There was endless knocking on the door, which we were not allowed to answer because there were people trying to serve him papers or looking for a car he was supposedly selling but drove for his own personal use. Policemen showed up multiple times. When driving in the car, no one was allowed to turn around and look if he spotted a cop behind us. There were no cell phones or answering machines, just a phone in the living room, tucked away inside its own black leather box. That same phone would be off limits for days on end, left off the hook, or unplugged from the wall by my dad.

In contrast, twice a year, my aunts, with Grandfather's permission, would make special arrangements at a clothing store in Brentwood called The Red Balloon. They would open just for us and all of our cousins in advance of their biennial sale. We could have whatever clothing we wanted from the shop. At the same time, my mom said she had just enough grocery money to get by, nothing extra. She hardly had enough to feed us hamburger every night, and made a full menu out of Spanish rice, chili and crackers, spaghetti, hot dogs, and macaroni and cheese. On Sundays, she would make fried chicken, but had to buy a whole chicken and cut it up.

Dad usually ate out and almost always came home late. He never drank, he never smoked, and he never did drugs because he was a control freak, but he was a sex addict who kept a large stash of pornography all over the house and cheated on my mom constantly.

I never saw my parents fight, but I could hear heated discussions in their bedroom even with their door closed. They usually happened because my Dad had shown up really late and my Mom would ask him where he had been.

"Not in front of the children," he would say.

She was upset but would have to be quiet. He wouldn't allow her to show any emotion while he worked his narcissistic magic and smoothed things over. My mother was miserable but played the part of dutiful Mormon wife to perfection by making her children her life. No one could possibly comprehend the magnitude of what she was forced to hide behind closed doors.

Mostly she kept quiet because, like everyone else, she was afraid to be on John Brown's bad side. Neighbors in the apartments on both sides and across the street filed complaints with the police department against my dad for destruction of property. He'd get in fights with people and deface their property by slashing their tires or taking spray paint and writing things on their walls. He was also charged with being a peeping tom after being caught on the roof watching women undress in the apartment next door. He did that all the time. I saw him do it myself.

In other words, you didn't want to mess with him.

My dad used to say to people, "I may not get you today, I may not get you tomorrow, I may not get you next week, but I will get you."

The State Board of Equalization, however, was not scared of my dad. In 1977, they brought a suit against him for $30,000 for unpaid resale taxes on the cars he was selling. In March 1979, John came home with papers for my mom to quitclaim the house over to Grandfather because the Board of Equalization was going to attach the house. He told her that if she didn't sign it, they would take the house, so she signed it.

She had no other choice.

# RIPPLE EFFECT

Even though we went about living our lives as though all was normal—me with my traveling church singing group, cheerleading, Girl Scouts, sports, and busy social life, and my brothers and sisters with their own versions of the same—my father's bad behavior left its mark.

Brad loved being a Boy Scout and liked to play sports, especially baseball. He fished, camped, and played outdoors. The neighborhood kids liked him, but he wasn't very social. One day, he stabbed a can of spray paint with a screwdriver and covered himself in green paint. My mom had to take him to the emergency room. He also had a penchant for setting fires and blowing things up.

*What little boy doesn't?* my mom told herself, but she worried. When Jason was little, he got a scar after chasing Brad through the house. Brad ran from the lanai up into the living room and slammed the door behind him. Jason ran into it, hitting the glass with his head and splitting his forehead open.

It was typical "roughhousing" and Brad was your average boy. However, Mom's fears were justified when it came to Jason.

In 1972, in kindergarten at Bonner Private School, I said F….you. I was praying it was my aunt's day for pick up, because I knew Mom would have let me have it. Lucky for me, my aunt did pull up at the end of the day. I didn't get into any trouble. Dad never used bad words until after my mom left him, so they knew I must have learned the word from the boy at school who I said dared me to do it.

When I was eight, I took my prized yellow Schwinn to get candy at the Rexall on Westwood Boulevard. As I was parking my bike, I saw a couple of guys drawing graffiti on the bus stop. I didn't have a lock and was kind of concerned, so I leaned the bike in a way that I could see it from inside the store. As I was checking out, I saw the tire moving. I dropped everything and ran out just as one of the guys climbed onto my bike.

I chased him past Smith's grocery into the alley holding onto the book rack on the back of the bike with a tight grip, screaming "my bike, my bike!" at the top of my lungs. The guy who worked nearby at Peterson's flower shop recognized me as John Brown's daughter. He watched me follow the thief into a nearby alley, so he jumped into his flower delivery Pinto to block the exit so the guy couldn't get away.

"Here you go, BRAT!" the thief shouted.

As the guy threw my bike at me, the delivery guy tackled him to the ground and held him there until the police showed up.

The LAPD loaded my beloved Schwinn into the trunk and drove me home. As it happened, my Sunday school teacher had been across the street and saw the whole thing. She told the whole class about how brave I'd been in the face of danger and gave me a book about courage with a personal letter inside.

I was fierce, feisty, and proud of it. My rebellious nature would lead me into a lot of trouble along the way, but there was enough happening around me that I didn't have to look far to find it.

It was late on a Friday night. My mom, brothers, and sister were already sound asleep. Like my father, I was, and am, a night owl, and was watching a show on the small Sony TV he had won on a game show. The Browns loved to try out for, and appear on, shows like Hollywood Squares. Somehow, I was the only kid with a television in my room and the only person in the family whose bedroom faced the front of the house.

I heard shouting, scuffling, and grunts outside. I opened my door, tiptoed into the living room, and peered through the drapes to see what was going on.

Dad was out front arguing with a strange man.

"I want my money," the man, wobbly and drunk, slurred.

My father gave him a shove. "Get the hell out of here."

"Not until you pay what you owe me…"

I was eight years old, and it wasn't the first time someone had come to the door looking for a car or cash Dad supposedly owed them. Still, I'd never seen anything like that before and was shocked and afraid as they took swings at each other. My fear turned to horror when I saw the man tumble down the stairs out of my sight. My father had pushed him down the flight of stairs onto the driveway.

An awful silence followed.

I ran back to my room so scared I pretended I was asleep listening to the car drive off into the dark. I waited for him to come back in, praying and trying to tell myself I hadn't seen what I thought I'd seen, but fell asleep long before he came home.

I never said a word about it to anyone—not to my mother or even my siblings.

After all, I had already been trained to keep my mouth shut where my dad's extracurriculars were concerned.

# FAMILY COMPOUND
## 1979-1982

"Iwant the whole family surrounding me until my last days," Grandfather announced one day. At the time, he lived in a large Spanish style home in Westwood; we were on Malcolm in West L.A.; Aunt Brooke was on the other side of the Mormon temple; and Aunt Sherri and her family lived nearby in Bel Air. Even though we were all fairly close to each other, he wanted to have the whole family around him. He claimed it was what he'd always wanted.

I feel like Grandfather should have said something more along the lines of, *I want all the grandkids to grow up on the same street; I want everybody to be together, surrounded by family love and support,* but no one asked what I thought.

He decided Laguna Beach was the place to go. We had two big family motorhomes, so all of us—my grandparents, aunts, uncles, and cousins—packed into them and headed down toward Orange County. We toured a group of houses that were being built on a cul-de-sac overlooking the ocean on Hillview Drive. Laguna was just getting developed and at $500-$600,000 each, they were some of the priciest homes in the area.

Just what he wanted for his family.

One of my aunts called my mom and announced they were all moving to Laguna. Mom was never asked if she wanted to move, just told it was happening and which house would be hers. Once again, Grandfather went ahead and paid the down payment. Mom was sent down to Orange County to employ her design talents and select the tile, stained glass for the kitchen and master bath, carpet, light fixtures, blinds, wallpaper, hardwood, and drapes. She chose the exterior brick work and the landscaping for what was to be our family home. We moved in July of 1979. Later, Grandfather would state that he never intended the Hillview house to belong to John and Jane because John couldn't afford it. In the meantime, Mom was told that the mortgage on the Hillview house was $2000 per month and that Grandfather would take the "rent" out of the proceeds from the Malcolm Avenue house when it sold (which it eventually did for $265,000). As it turned out, the mortgage was actually $1000 per month.

Brad was thirteen, I was eleven, Jason was ten, and Carrie was eight. Grandfather and Grandmother moved into a house in the middle of the street. We lived across the way at 2240 Hillview Drive. My dad's sister Sherri, her husband Bob, and their five kids lived next door to us. My dad's younger sister Brooke, her husband, and their four kids lived around the corner behind my grandparents. In my teenage years, I renamed it Hellview Drive.

At first, life in Laguna Beach was peaceful—relatively speaking—and definitely full of activity. We went to church every Sunday for three hours. There were social events including progressive church dinner parties, sports, and family activities galore. There were church camps in the summer, Eagle Scout merit badges for the boys to earn, and endless sports. I still had my beloved singing and dancing group, the Songsmiths, which involved lots of traveling. I was on the tennis team and Carrie was a tennis star, (my dad had high hopes of her turning pro). She was coached by Robert Lansdorp, Tracy Austin's coach. My mom drove her back and forth to private lessons in Pacific Palisades.

We played with all of our cousins and had Christmas Eve at our grandparents' with elaborate meals and lots of presents. Every holiday was an event on our street. Everything was 100% *happy family*. Fake, but in my eyes, fine.

One weekend, soon after we moved into our compound, Grandfather had invited everyone we knew from Westwood to come for a party on our street to show off our beautiful homes. During the party, with all the visitors filling the street, and walking in and out of houses enjoying refreshments, a Laguna Beach patrol car started making the turn onto Hillview Drive. Of course, Dad was the first to spot it and ran up to the patrol car before it made its way into view of the others. My older brother and a neighbor friend (who, ironically, grew up to become a judge and had to recuse himself from a case involving my dad) were in the back. The police officer explained that there'd been an incident that involved fishing and fishing weights off the famous Aliso Beach pier in Laguna. Somehow, Dad got them out of there without anyone really noticing—of course he did.

Grandfather arranged a job for Dad with a man from the church. He was to turn in his gas receipts for the job but he was adding on personal gas, so the guy let him go. Dad was also doing weekends in jail because of the Board of Equalization court decision. Despite his legal issues related to selling cars, he kept a Volkswagen Rabbit from 1977 to 1981. He told the owner, a single attractive woman who lived at the bottom of our cul-de-sac, that he'd tried to sell it at auction but there were no takers. He'd, of course, disconnected the odometer and had been driving it constantly.

He always said to me, "Jami, possession is nine-tenths of the law."

Clearly, he lived by that motto.

We had the best bikes, tennis rackets, and *stuff*, but less and less money to live on. In my journal, I wrote: *I keep hearing my parents talk about money problems so I am going to try to earn my own money and buy what I need. I have earned $25 in one week. Moneybags Jami, my mom calls me.*

Despite the fact that Mormon parents are taught to avoid debt which spiritually burdens and can even ruin a family, Dad began to gamble more, often down in Mexico—sometimes winning big, and losing just as often. When money would appear, my mom was mortified, wondering, but never asking, where it had come from. Grandfather kept paying my father's way out of trouble. In December 1980, Grandfather became very alarmed because of a $14,750 gambling debt my father had accumulated, most likely on one of the big credit lines he had at the casinos. He was also borrowing heavily and taking out fake loans. When a loan shark threatened to harm us if the money wasn't paid back, we had to go live at my grandparents' house until they could get the money together to ensure our safety.

In November 1981, a marshal came to the house to serve Dad a warrant related to unpaid tickets on a leased car. He ran out the back door to avoid being served in front of the family. He was caught and given ten days over Christmas. Mom was told to tell the family he had gone to Texas on business. My mom visited him at the Orange County jail. The lawyer finally got him out at 8:00 PM on Christmas Eve. He'd served his jail time but was given a three-year probation for selling cars without a license.

By January 1981, my Grandparents read my mom the family will. It excluded my dad from ever receiving any cash but stated that his heirs would be taken care of. Mom was furious that Dad had put her in such a bad financial position through his recklessness, but glad her children wouldn't have to suffer for their father's sins.

Not those sins, anyway.

Through it all, Dad managed to maintain his paternalistic stronghold on her and especially us kids, something I would soon come to realize was yet another manifestation of the narcissistic sociopathic personality disorder he'd inherited from his father and had passed on down the line.

That same year, Dad became president of the Laguna Beach Little League. My dad liked coaching because he was in a position of control. He never allowed the kids to think for themselves. He told them where to go, directing them at all times. He wasn't teaching them. He was just controlling them and telling them what to do. He was a really aggressive coach and winning was the goal. Needless to say, the other parents eventually became concerned about his win at all cost strategies.

By April, Dad was ousted from coaching Little League because of unethical procedures and bad influence on the children of Laguna Beach. It didn't deter him from his aggressive behavior at sporting events, however. He would come to my tennis matches and stand by the fence on whatever side I was playing. Mouth cupped, he'd make comments and yell orders. It was all about winning and it stressed me out. When we played doubles at our daddy-daughter tennis tournaments, he would cheat. If a ball hit the baseline or came really close to the alley and it was clearly in, he'd insist it was out. A huge fight would ensue. It was utterly humiliating.

In May 1982, Dad talked his way into a job as the Laguna High School junior varsity assistant baseball coach. The parents in the booster club objected, so he was told by the principal that he wouldn't be paid but could volunteer. When the other coaches got wind of his hiring, they threatened to quit if he came on staff in any capacity.

My mom felt she had no choice but endure my dad's gambling, infidelity, and unscrupulous behavior. She not only witnessed him cheat people out of money but she also had to suffer the embarrassment of having him cut down a neighbor's bushes while they were on vacation or say nothing as he poisoned someone's tree that was blocking his view. My uncle Bob borrowed our hose without permission and didn't return it. When my uncle bought another one, my dad went over and cut it into little tiny pieces.

In September 1982, three years after we'd moved to the family compound on Hillview Drive, my parents returned from what was supposed to be an all-expenses paid Caribbean cruise (courtesy of Grandfather who won a lot of contests for large sales in the insurance business and sometimes sent his kids with their spouses). Dad had Brad go down to the canyon car lot Grandfather owned to meet potential buyers because he had lost his dealer's license due to his fraudulent schemes and was banned from selling cars. Brad was only fifteen at the time and my mom was horrified that he was trying to bring his son into his criminal activities and schemes. My mom knew she had to get John Brown out of her children's lives immediately. She had no money of her own, and she was scared, but it was time to act.

Mom hadn't yet told anyone she was planning to leave my dad. I was walking up the hill to catch a ride with my cousins to seminary one morning. I had just started my freshman year of high school and seminary was a bible study/youth program for kids grades 9-12. It started 1 ½ hours before school, Monday through Friday, and its purpose (or so it seemed to me) was to help us withstand the worldly temptations that came with being a teenager. Most of my cousins graduated from it with perfect attendance. I struggled from the beginning. I was not a morning person, and from what would soon reveal itself to be a very troubled home, and I had no intention of following rules like no bikini bathing suits.

As I was headed up the hill, highly irritated about having to go as the sun was barely rising, I saw a hooded figure running out from the side of the neighbor's house. (They had a Ferrari which we thought was cool, so we called them the *flashy* neighbors.) The hooded man ran across the street and headed to the main road. Seconds later, I heard screams from the house and the owner came running out. She said the alarm had been triggered and a man was trying to break into her baby boy's bedroom.

"We need to find out what direction he went to tell the police," I said.

As we ran to the top of Hillview, the man, now in a truck he'd parked across the street in the dirt off Park Avenue, was directly in front of me. He rolled down his tinted driver's side window and out came the end of a gun. It looked like a rifle but sounded like a handgun as shots whizzed by my head. I yelled at my neighbor to get down and she proceeded to roll down the asphalt street. I hunched and ran. As I turned the corner onto our street, I hid behind the wheel well of a parked car. Panting and scared out of my mind, my mom and dad came out on the balcony.

"Jami! Jami!!" my mom screamed over and over. She thought I'd been shot.

The next thing I knew, my dad was in our truck flying past me in pursuit of the shooter. He tried to run the guy off the road and ended up crashing his vehicle, but the guy got away. In the aftermath of being shot at as a high school freshman, I concluded that our neighbors had to be drug dealers. Why else would someone break into their house a 6:00 AM? We never found out for sure, but my dad applied for some kind of Crime Stoppers reward for his efforts and got a check for $2000.

A check my parents would fight over, almost to the death.

It was a sunny Saturday a week or two later when Mom asked me to go across the street to the tennis courts at Thurston Junior High school and hit some balls with her. She said needed to talk to me which was weird given how quiet and non-confrontational she usually was. The moment we stepped out onto the tennis courts together, she said, "Your dad and I are getting a divorce."

In the Mormon religion, families are forever. You don't get divorced. I knew my parents fought sometimes but I didn't understand what was really going on at all. My whole world shattered. Everything was an illusion and a façade and it had all come crumbling down.

"Why? Why?" I cried, bawling my head off.

"I'm really sorry," she said.

"It's okay, Mom," I finally said through my tears, but only to make her feel better. "I have a lot of friends whose parents are divorced."

I'll never forget walking back with her, still sobbing, and painfully aware that life as I knew it was over. LDS teachings state, "the disintegration of the family will bring upon individuals, communities, and nations, the calamities foretold by ancient and modern prophets."

Neither of us could have imagined how much worse it would get.

# WAR OF THE BROWNS
## SEPTEMBER 1982–MARCH 1983

Dad spent the next week trying to talk Mom out of getting divorced. The more she refused to listen to his pleas to stay, the crazier he got. When he realized she wasn't going to be talked out of her decision, he took my siblings aside and said, "Your mother is destroying our family. She's divorcing me and leaving you. Don't talk to her. Don't interact with her."

Jason and Carrie were young and compliant. Brad knew it was best for him to play the game. As the defiant, rebellious one, I wasn't going to be controlled by Dad or swayed by his blatant lies. He wasn't about to move out and Mom's attorney had instructed her not to leave under any circumstances.

"Jane," the attorney said. "If you leave the house, you're never going to get back in again."

From that point on, things went from horrible to worse.

My dad took all Mom's belongings out of their room and threw everything into my bedroom, which I shared with Carrie. He then took all of Carrie's stuff out and put it in the big master bathroom and had her sleep in there. He also took the keys to Mom's car so she had to borrow one from her sister who lived north of Los Angeles in Agoura Hills.

Mom got a job as a playground assistant at Top of the World, my sister's elementary school. Carrie was instructed to completely ignore my mother whenever she saw her there. Dad picked Carrie up every day for lunch because he didn't want her to go to lunchtime P.E. because Mom was on the playground. Only my cousin who went there as well was still kind to Mom.

While she was at work, Dad did things like have the telephone shut off. He also removed pictures from the walls and took all of Mom's belongings—cosmetics, jewelry, personal childhood scrapbooks, divorce correspondence—anything that had meaning to her. If she was reading a novel, he took that. He tried to break her down and strip her of everything so that she would come back to him.

My mom said she wanted the antique jewelry out of the safe. John wasn't about to let her have it, even though it was from her mom and aunt. She was so angry, she grabbed the Crime Stoppers check that had just been mailed to the house and walked away. Dad was livid. Mom went over to Grandfather's house hoping he would arbitrate their dispute. My stoic, unemotional grandfather instructed her to give John the check back or he would not give her the jewelry— never mind it wasn't his. Mom returned the check as advised and John gave my mother her jewelry back, but he'd popped the largest diamond out of one of the rings.

My dad would steal from anyone, but if someone messed with something that was his, he became a force to be reckoned with. Worse, Dad proceeded to absolutely brainwash my siblings. He bribed them to be on Team Dad by buying them everything they wanted—new clothes, shoes, sports equipment and the "prized" BMX bikes which later became their main form of transportation. Brad was sixteen and my dad gave him someone's lifted four-wheel drive truck that had been featured in a magazine (even though it wasn't around for very long). To me, it felt like Jason and Carrie, already subservient, had become Dad's minions.

Because I sided with my mother, the four of them made both of our lives a living hell. Nobody spoke to anybody. Jason and Carrie stole my stuff and spit at Mom and me because Dad told them to. The house was divided into two enemy camps and it was survival of the fittest. My mom and I stayed in my room so Dad would turn the heater up at night to ninety degrees to sweat us out of the house. We locked the door, so he removed the door to my bedroom entirely. I was playing varsity tennis so he stole my varsity letter jacket and my tennis racket so I couldn't play in my tournament. We had to hide everything. Mom put the keys to her sister's car she'd borrowed under her pillow because Dad would send Jason and Carrie to steal our stuff at night. At one point, they even TP'd our room.

Once, while my mom took a shower, they found the car keys. Jason opened the car and took all the personal belongings she had been hiding in the trunk. Eventually, the keys went missing entirely and Mom had to borrow a friend's car to drive to my aunt's house in Los Angeles for a set of duplicates. My mom had written letters every Sunday for fifteen years to my Grandma detailing every small detail of our childhood which she was saving as a keepsake for us. My Dad took them out of her trunk and burned them.

Dad had instructed my siblings to refuse to eat anything Mom cooked for them. If Mom brought home any food for the two of us, he would throw it out. If I made brownies, he'd fill the pan up with water and ruin them. He did everything he could think of to mentally break us down.

One day, after work, Mom was heading out to her car with some personal items she planned to put to take to her sister's for safekeeping. She found my dad leaning against the car, blocking the trunk.

"Get off my car," she said, her arms full.

He wouldn't budge.

There had never been any physicality between them before, but she felt she had no choice and kicked him in the shin. "Move."

My mom was five foot nothing and 100 pounds and while she'd definitely kicked him, she'd done so wearing a light pair of tennis shoes. In response, he reached out and slapped her in the face with his open palm. Her head spun and she saw stars.

Carrie and I heard shouting and came out in time to see my mom fly onto the ground. We ran off screaming and crying to Aunt Brooke's to tell her Dad hit Mom. What the family did about that information I can't be sure, but the lawyer told Mom to take a photo. She was embarrassed about going to work the next day with a black eye.

Two days later, the attorney got a restraining order.

Because he had to stay 500 feet from the house, Dad couldn't live with my grandparents. While he later told the court a pathetic tale of sleeping in his car and suffering through the cold, wet, California winter, we all knew Grandfather had put him up somewhere. He was only gone for two days—*heaven* according to Mom—before he walked back into the house, threw papers at her, and said he'd gotten the restraining order lifted.

Already in retribution mode overdrive, he'd managed to master-mind a slander campaign against Mom with the psychologist his at-torney set up for him who reported:

*Mr. John Brown and three of his children were interviewed on September 23, 1982. The family had been referred by Mr. Brown's attorney due to pending divorce, custody, and living arrangements liti-gation. At the time that the family was interviewed a restraining issue had been issued against Mr. Brown by his wife, for reported spousal abuse. This examiner, after having interviewed Mr. Brown, adminis-tering psychological testing, and having interviewed his children both with him and alone, had concluded that he was not a danger to him-self or others, furthermore, Mr. Brown and his children had reported a long history of abusive behavior by the mother towards the children and the husband. In the examiner's September 23, 1982 report, he had recommended family counseling for the Brown family, had recom-mended at least a physical examination to rule out physical health rea-sons for the mother's temperamental difficulties, and had suggested that he contact Child Protective Services for assistance should the children's welfare be in danger.*

In truth, there was no *history* of abusive behavior on my mom's part. Once, back in Los Angeles, she'd backhanded me for mouthing off. I had braces at the time and my cheek got caught on one of the brackets causing my mouth to bleed. My mother was so horrified, she vowed to never use any form of corporal punishment again.

The facts didn't stop my father from reporting that my mother was completely out of control:

*...[father] depicts himself as a conciliator, protecting his children, while his wife, who suffers constant headaches, flies off the handle unpredictably. Jane "can't take the pressure" and has a ten year history of taking Valium and Excedrin.*

Mom took those drugs because she suffered from migraines.

The psychologist noted that "[John] acknowledged past legal difficulties relating to his car business but denied any [history] of violence in or outside of the family," and found my father to be "likable and not hostile." When the conversation turned to my dad's, "considerable legal difficulties" highlighting his expulsion from BYU, he said, "They hung me on a technicality."

Dad was given tests for depression, paranoia, hypomania, psychopathic deviation, and hysteria. The "animal responses" on the inkblot test showed a tendency toward impulsiveness, but somehow, he had given no violent or inappropriate responses and showed no evidence of severe mood disorder, psychosis, or violence. As a result, the restraining order was lifted less than thirty days after it had been granted.

It was war and we were losing badly. Mom called a counselor in the bishopric who came and got us immediately. We went to live with an older church member at her townhouse in Laguna Niguel so we'd be safe until the church could figure out where to put us.

As we were leaving, my dad said to me, "If you go with your mother, you're going to wish you hadn't."

The therapist saw my dad a few days after he was back in the house and reported the following:

*According to Mr. Brown, the restraining order had been lifted, he is back at the house, but his wife was now living with his parents across the street; the 14-year-old daughter Jami was living with his sister. According to Mr. Brown, his wife had broken down hysterically when he was allowed back in the house, became quite upset, and moved out. According to both father and son, Mr. Brown and the children are getting along well, showing cooperation with daily household chores, with minimal conflict. Concerning the issue of possible physical abuse, Jason related that "on September 26th that Saturday afternoon about 5:30, I was in my room. She hit me with her fist across the nose and across the right eye and I ran out the door. She chased me and shook me and told me I'd never see my dad again." According to Mr. Brown, "My wife is always violent to the kids, can't express affection. The marriage won't make it if she doesn't pull together."*

*The discussion then turned towards possible living arrangements in the eventuality of separation and divorce. "I earn only about $1400 a month and I can't afford two homes. I plan to move into a three bedroom apartment in Corona del Mar and have the children living with me, I'm up with them in the morning and home with them from 3:00 PM on. Carrie, the youngest, is terrified of her mom, and if the court orders her to live with her mom, I'm sure she'll run away. She has nightmares of her mom going to beat her."*

*Both the examiner and Mr. Brown contacted Child Protective Services in order to report physical abuse, based upon what Mr. Brown and Jason reported. Since the children were currently living with Mr. Brown, and in no immediate danger of physical abuse, Child Protective Services stated that they would await any outcome of the conciliation court recommendation... However, the examiner is of the opinion that the children's welfare may be at risk should there be prolonged contact between mother and children without some kind of counseling...*

My mom hadn't hit Jason, and never told him he'd never see his dad again. He had no intention of moving out of the house and into an apartment. He had, however, managed to convince the psychologist that Mom was the crazy one, not him.

On September 28, 1982, my mom told me that Dad came up to the elementary school and made a huge scene in front of fifty kids in the bus line by talking about Mom's character and saying all kinds of crazy stuff.

Dad was not about to allow my siblings to reestablish their connection with Mom and directed Carrie 11, Jason 13, and Brad 16, to write letters to the court about what a good parent he was and how horrible and abusive mom was in "their own words." Of course, the words they wrote came directly from him. Their spelling and grammatical errors made the letters seem legit:

*Mr. Smith,*

*My dad has been taking good care of me. He cook all of are food. And we clean the house and does all of the dish and the laundry.*

*My mom is very mean and hateful to me and my brothers. She cuses and calls my daddy names in front of us. And she won't let us have the heater on at night. I am very cold and she always turns it off. She is Allways blaming my dad on things that he does not do. She does not talk to me if she does she runs my father down and she screams at me all the time. I do not know what is wrong with my mom but I am afraid of her because she might hit me. At school all she does at school is stare at me.*

*Selver times she grabed me and shook me around. I wish I could go to another school for I won't be afraid of her. My brothers and I try to stay away from my mom and sister. Because they always screams and yells and cause problems. My dad never say anything bad about my mom. I don't want to live with my mother at all because she is not fair to my. She bought Jami all these clothes and not me or my brothers. My and my sister do not get along at all.*

*Carrie Brown*

*Mr. Smith,*

*When I heard about the divorce I was very upset my dad sat down with me and explained it and I understood. What was going to happen to me.*

*My mother never took time to explain it to me or my brother or my sister Carrie when my dad was to be out of the house. I told my mother that I wanted him to come back and live with me. She became very mad at me and started hiting me and shaking me I ran over to my grandfather's house and they made me feel better. She always hits across the face and loses control.*

*She swears at my dad when we are around and puts my dad down in front of us. She called my dad a faggot the other night when we were in the garage my dad closed the garage and angered her. We try to stay away from her whenever possible. I broke out crying and my dad said not to worry that my mother didn't really mean it. My dad is always nice to my mother but she is always mean and cruel to him. He always tells us to be nice to her and she just having a hard time right now.*

*Mother is always causing problems and blames my dad for doing things. She blamed my dad for getting into her car one morning. I got* into her car I found the keys in her room. My dad got mad at me and punished me for it. My mother has been taking things out of the house and they never come back. Yesterday me and Carrie saw her taking one of my dad's briefcases and putting it in the trunk of her car, we told my dad and he said not to worry. … be so hateful. Mother lets my sister Jami call my dad names and be hateful to him. And my dad never gets mad at her. I just wished that they would leave and not bother us anymore. My dad, Brad, Carrie and I get along just fine none of us can get along with Jami at all

Jason Brown

Mr. Smith,

I am writing this letter to you because my dad asked me to so you can understand what is going on. First, I want you to know that I get along with my father very well and I love him very much. I do not get along with my mother at all she is very mean to me, my father, and Carrie and Jason. I also don't get along with my sister Jami at all. She is a real brat she has a very nasty mouth.

My dad, Carrie, Jason and I have been getting along great. Every morning, my father gets up and fixes breakfast for us, gets us off to school. At night we have dinner together and after dinners we go and have family pray. On Monday nights we have family pray and we have an activity.

My mother swears at my father in front of my brother and sister and I. She uses bad language which we aren't supposed to use. She use such words as you fucking son of a bitch and other. She trys to run are father down in front of us and tells us all these lies about him, She also loses her temper very easily. I will try to talk it out with her but she goes crazy and tries to hit me in the face, She also does this with Jason and Jason is very much afraid of her.

My mother ignores us. She never talks to us and never cooks us food it's like she doesn't care for us anymore.

Jami wastes a lot of food, She'll sometimes will open a can of food take a few bites and pass it down the drain. She does this with everything. One morning I was eating breakfast and had some grape nuts the doorbell rang and I went to answer it when I came back the box was empty Jami had pass the grape nuts down the sink and she had run out the side door.

Mother and Jami complain about there is never any food around the house when they waste it.

They never buy any food for themselves. We have to hide our food so they won't waste it and throw it away in the garbage. They who never clean up after themselves. They leave the kitchen a mess. We clean the kitchen and keep it straight. We also do the laundry every day.

One thing that was totally uncalled for was when my mother turned on my father about my sister. Carrie didn't want to sleep with my mother because she is afraid of my mother. So she wants to sleep with my dad. So my mother comes in and started to yell and just went on yelling.

She also ransacks the stuff in the house she goes through everything in the house and takes what she wants.

The other day my brother saw my mother take something out of the house and stick it in her trunk. My father went to find what she took also the other day my mother comes up to me and says I'm going to get your dad kick out of the house and get custody of the house and the children.

*I think that the best thing that could happen is that my mother and Jami go their own way and Carrie, Jason, and I go with my father.*

*Brad Brown*

The counselor interviewed Brad, Carrie, and Jason alone, and with Dad, who did everything he could to make sure he was in the room with them. He found my siblings to be *quite close and affection-ate with their dad.... Clinical observations suggest a warm, spontaneous relationship with Dad and one another. All are involved with sports, do well in school, relate well to others, and despite the current trauma, do not appear to suffer psychological disturbance.*

Because of my Mom's fervent objections over what was being said about her, the judge ordered Dad to meet with a different court-appointed psychologist.

The second psychologist objected to dad's attorney's intention to have the first psychologist attend his sessions with dad on the grounds that:

*Accepted practice determines that the psychologist (whether court appointed or not) performs psychodiagnostics interviews and psychodi-agnostics testing with the patient, no other persons being present. The presence of another distorts the psychologist-patient relationship in ways that science doesn't know how to measure: it introduces an extraneous and uncontrolled variable and thereby changes the atmosphere for the examination. The presence of another can serve to constrain the patient's response to questions and his or her responses to test times. It can also constrain the examiner and inhibit the usual and customary psychodi-agnostics evaluation.*

My dad showed up for the session but told the psychologist he couldn't afford counseling and didn't need it anyway because he'd been counseled by his Mormon bishop and would do anything to make his marriage work because, "We don't believe in divorce."

The new psychologist felt the mental health evaluation given by the first counselor was not thorough enough to conclude that John didn't suffer from a disorder. He noted that that the letters my siblings wrote at Dad's prompting, *calls into serious question whether or not he is interested in the welfare of the children, and whether he can tolerate, let alone nurture and support, a positive relationship between the children and their mother… He involves the children as weapons in his fight.*

He proceeded to have a conjoint meeting with just the siblings:

*Sessions with Brad, Jami, Jason, and Carrie Brown—December 18 and 10, 1982*

*For the first session, Jami arrived first, by herself. Exactly at the appointed hour, Brad and Jason arrived together. Brad and Jami began to converse immediately. At seven minutes after the hour, with my consulting room door open awaiting the arrival of Carrie, John (the father) opened the outer door, saw Brad, and called him to go get Carrie. I called Brad back and asked John to bring Carrie (where he had left her, I do not know). Jason said he had to go to the bathroom and left briefly. Carrie arrived one minute later.*

*The parents had been instructed to not be present in my office. In another attempt to manipulate and control, John called Brad out of inner office. His other manipulations are documented elsewhere.*

69

*I then asked the children to go back two years in time and tell me what family life was like. Jason began, followed by Brad, Jami, and Carrie. They indicated they were a family then, one that got along, with children obeying parents. The children then described the onset of the arguments and the parents sleeping separately. Jami notes that the love between the four children began to change and Jason stated that the children had never gotten along but that he, Carrie, and Brad get along better. Brad pointed out that Jami took mother's side, the other three father's side.*

*I found Carrie and Jason taking issue with everything Jami uttered.: they were poised for battle no matter what she said. I focused very strongly on Jason and Carrie as the most disturbed in this respect and the two most needing help to resolve the problems. Brad did not like me singling out Jason and Carrie, and thirty-five minutes into the hour, stood up and led Jason and Carrie out of the office.*

*It is apparent to me that Jason and Carrie have been trained to fight with Jami. I think Brad and Jami actually care less about the fighting and could resolve their differences fairly quickly. Jason and Carrie appear to me to be extremely upset and negative at this time. Brad as eldest perhaps feels he has to come to their defense, but he used poor judgement in interrupting the session. One wonders if he had received instructions about this or whether he was exercising his own judgment.*

"I'm not sure how much longer I can stand the game being played," Mom told the court, worrying about the effects of my dad's emotionally scarring behavior on all of us. "I hope that the former loving relationship between my children and myself can be restored, despite (John's) attempts to destroy it."

The problem was, my dad didn't follow rules, he took whatever it was he wanted, and like he always said and truly believed, "Possession is nine-tenths of the law."

He wasn't about to let my mom win, and neither was the Brown family.

My mom's mother, my beloved pistol of a grandma from Texas, whose motto in life was, "Put on a little lipstick and everything will be okay," was so upset by the circumstances surrounding the divorce that she stood up to Grandmother and Grandfather and the powerful Brown clan by writing the following letter:

*Wrangell, Alaska*
*Feb. 18, 1983*

*Dear Gen and Bernie,*
*It is with sadness that I write you, having considered my thoughts with much prayer over many weeks since the last time I wrote.*

*It is very difficult to try to lead another person's life. And even worse in the sight of our Heavenly Father to be a pillar to one who is unsightly in His eyes.*

*Only once has Jane told an untruth. When she was about nine. She opened the refrigerator door and the sugar bowl which was on top (and not far enough back) fell and spilled sugar on the floor. Each of the girls was asked who spilled the sugar - none would confess. Then her daddy saw sugar in her hair and he knew Jane did it. She cried and said when she opened the door it fell.*

*You folks have spent so much time believing John's lies about Jane; never once asking Jane if it were the truth. Evidently you wanted to believe John, which is good, however believing the wrong person but "you didn't want to take sides," so you said.*

*Why, Bernie, when Jane came to you before last Easter and told you she couldn't put up with anymore of John's ways and wanted out, did you tell her "think it over and I will stand behind you whatever your decision." Then when she came to you again, you turned your back on her. You, her only friend? What a friend! Even poor, poor Gen said, "She could have done it another way," and I said, "What other way Gen?" "Well," she said, "I don't want to talk about it." No even she didn't want to hear the truth.*

*I wonder which one of your daughters would have lived with a John Brown for 17 years? And why would you or the Lord want her punished like that. Oh, you wouldn't stand behind Jane because she wasn't your daughter - you were going to make her stay with John Brown!! And if she wasn't going to stay, you would punish her by helping John Brown take the children from her. Yes, you took the children. You backed his lies with money; you stole the children's love from their mother because you didn't see that the John Brown you were financing told the children the truth about everything; instead you sanctioned his twisting the truth until it looked like their mother didn't love them, these poor innocent babes; because she didn't want to live with John Brown; his unsightly ways, his bad influence on the children, his tearing her health down, his forcing her to tell telephone callers he wasn't in, even to his own dad, and if she didn't there would be no grocery* money. You are saying, "I don't believe that." Well ask Jane - for it is the truth. Jane is not made up of untruths, cheating and stealing. This is why 17 years has been so hard on her.

Many times John has asked me, "Do you think Jane would leave me?" and then he adds, "I think she would stay for the kids." Why did he ask me this if he was living a righteous life? He wasn't and he knows he wasn't or he wouldn't have had any ideas of her leaving.

From the time Jane was advised, after John was forced to leave BYU for stealing, by Faculty to <u>not</u> marry John Brown (but because of his glib salesmanship - he repented and would never do it again) (Ha!) she consented to marry <u>this Elder</u>. On in the time they were married less than two years, he John Brown, trespassed the Lord's commandment and stole kitchen-ware from the Pasadena Savings and Loan in Pasadena - when I went to put up his bond there. John Brown's thieving was still a part of his life. Then, you two, Laura and Brooke came to Texas for Jami Dee's blessing. While at Church as Gen and I sat side by side, I said to Gen, "Before you leave I wish you would tell John you loved him," she retorted in haughty manner and said, "Why, does he have a problem?" I was dumbfounded that a mother would have such an air of indifference, unconcern, of not giving of love! John Brown had a hard time as a child convincing his parents he needed to be wanted, needed their love; too, being the middle child of five children it was difficult; so turning to other things for attention became a way of life with him. And this is when his problems began. He told me once, "I love you more than my own mother." I was horrified at his statement and said, "John, don't ever say that again, your mother should always be first; I appreciate your *love, but she comes first." In those days John was like a son to me; I loved him dearly and could feel his longing to have motherly love. Jane was the middle child too; having a sister older and one younger; we were close - she never worried about not being loved.*

*As John Brown was asked by you to leave Texas - come to California be a partner in the insurance business; they left Texas, rented out their house, I had given as a graduation present when she graduated from BYU, and proceeded in faith to California to the downfall or failing illusions of great things working with the "Brown's Incorporated." However it doesn't have a "happy ending" nor did it have a "happy beginning." Each time I visited the children 2 or 3 times a year, I wondered at the "poor progress" of this financial state. (They had their household of furniture, a new Chevrolet and an antique model T) to begin with hauled from Texas. Each time I visited, John would say, "I can't work with my dad; he will not pay me my insurance commissions even — he still owes me $5000.00 from the first few months I was here." They were not getting ahead, there was little money for groceries - no money for clothes, Jane made her dresses and got the children "used clothing at garage sales." I went to garage sales with Jane I was there — she never had over $2 or $3 to spend. Life with John has not been easy! Nor one to be proud of! John was never home with Jane and the children in the evenings — he <u>managed</u> to have appointments or outside interests. He says she wouldn't cook. I wonder how many times a wife puts dinner on the table and the husband doesn't come home to eat with her and the children — he is too busy. (Too busy doing what?) Not too busy making money but too busy spending it - that is gambling, or whatever.*

*Jane has raised her little children almost alone as John got up be-tween 9:30am and 10am, then was gone till late hours at night 10pm-11pm or later with an occasional return home for a few minutes. The children haven't been around John, their father, like children should have been during their growing up years - it has been Jane, who raised her children.*

*Since last Easter when they came back to California did John Brown realize that Jane was serious about dissolving their one-sided marriage after he had run her down, made fun, showed and encouraged disre-spect for [her] in front of the children... And only then did he decide to have family home evening with the children and began telling the children, "Your mother doesn't love you or she would attend family home evening." While I was there the few days in October, John said we're having family home evening - due to the friction (of the past 5-6 months) I didn't attend. It was a flippant farce in the face of my Heavenly Father. The one meal he, John Brown, allowed my grand-children to eat with me, he ended up in a rage at the table - the meal last 10 minutes. Also, when he was in court he ordered that I leave the house. (I had only intended to be there 6 days.) If I didn't agree to he said he would evict me. Of course I had come 1600 miles from Alaska to see Jane and the children and to try to talk to you two, which I was unable to do either as soon you barred their door and ran to and from behind it, peeking out, never asking us what we wanted or asking us in. (This is another instance of your not wanting to take sides - not face the truth about the state of affairs). But taking John Brown's side and scheming to try schemes to take Jane's children from her. Since Jane has been in the family for over 17 years and is and has received this kind*

75

*of vindication, there is little the other in-laws have to look forward to if they in any way do not conform to the Brown's edicts. It was quite shocking to learn you have requested John's family be taken off the family group insurance as the psychiatrist's tests began which were ordered by the court. I can't imagine your vindictiveness against but as you told us you weren't taking sides of Jane. I am sure there is a punishment for such antics and the rancor that John Brown and his supporters have demonstrated.*

*John Brown has been most vicious with those he dealt with. Cheating - this is stealing, lying taking advantage of anyone he could; his business and personal ethics have been those anyone would be ashamed of, let alone his own family. But this, Bernie, you have been behind all these years. Is this your method of getting ahead; taking advantage of anyone you could to gain materially?*

*It has been a costly fight for Jane's family to fight for her children; the children she has given her life to bring in this world and raise (by herself). We are a poor hardworking family compared to the "Bernie Brown Clan." We don't dwell on manipulations to gain worldly gains - we work. Well maybe you are saying we are just not as smart as you; you are right! We aren't in the underworld of life and I thank my Heavenly Father that those magnetic powers of the destroyer have not invaded our family. Just remember "Honesty and Truth" will always win out.*

*Besides your helping John Brown illegally, by <u>manipulations</u> and <u>payoffs</u> (you wonder how I can state <u>payoff</u> - John Brown went to Carrie's* school on <u>*Friday before Court on Monday*</u> *and had the records of the children changed to <u>his</u> guardianship - the Judge or Court had not made that decision until the <u>following Monday</u> - "PAYOFF," now you have indulged into <u>fake</u> IOUs. These IOUs are so phony that even a child can see through them. Bernie, how can you present these animated cartoons of money loaned to John Brown? You are only trying to establish that John has through the years borrowed money from you; eating up their profit they realized out of selling the Malcolm house - plus the $10,000 of Jane's money from selling her Pasadena home. Bernie you are a "smart business man!" There is no way a "smart business man" has $10,000 to $20,000 of cash lying around loose that could be drawing interest somewhere. This would be idiotic! Neither would a "smart businessman" lend cash to anyone, (let alone a "son" who isn't even trusted in his parents' house when they are not there and as John said his father was willing him over $1,000,000 in cars - stashed all over California but he will not be willed or have anything to do with "<u>Cash</u>" without having a cancelled check for it; what a phony set up of IOUs. You have even put an IOU that was bought and paid for while Jane was teaching in Texas. Bernie, how can you lie about all the money you say John owes you, just to <u>"cheat and steal"</u> from Jane? You might have given John a little money - especially the $13,000 gambling debt of 1981 but Bernie, you and Gen aren't stupid enough to cheat your other children out of an equal amount that you haven't given John. So why are you "<u>stealing</u>" from Jane?*

*You have been planning a long time to have your records in a position that Jane would never be able to have anything. How despicable! Jane does not want your money; Jane only wants her part. Are you persecuting*

*Jane for marrying John and rearing yours and mine grandchildren? This isn't just! Or didn't you want him back on your hands?*

*This was your idea to sell their Malcolm house and turn the profit over to you - move them to the Brown Empire - control their money - invest it - let the profit from their Malcolm house be invested in the Hillview house - and balance invested for interest. I know you are a real "intellect" when it comes to "investing and covering up." In a sense this is business, however when it comes to downright cheating or stealing from someone, that is degrading. There is still $30,000 against John Brown for failure to pay his car taxes/fees - so how can you show money loaned for this?*

*Too, it was very smart of you to borrow on Jane and John's Hillview house to the tune of $65,000 (from one of your other businesses) so that you can add another not invested and $65,000 of indebtedness trying to show poverty; my, my, what a bunch of crooks/thieves! I hope your other children have their homes in their names. I would hate to see their houses sold out from under them - they have much too high principles to be treated uncouthly.*

*Your whole little Hillview Empire (though I'm sure Gen's <u>intent</u> was above reproach in the beginning) is a shameful enterprise. All houses bought in your name, rented out, you took advantage of <u>appreciation</u>, <u>interest</u>, <u>insurance</u>, <u>taxes</u>, <u>gardener</u>, <u>maintenance</u>, and of course even the <u>furniture</u>...*

*(page destroyed here) ...trumpeted as company*

*<u>(page destroyed here)</u> ...off for the houses. Oh you had it figured down to the gnat's heel, exempt yourself from paying taxes. So through*

*this outlandish process you set up, Jane and John (after you reaped the benefits of your tax deductions) could not owe more than $2500.00 a year on house payments. Now where do you get all this money from their house has eroded away. John Brown was earning only $1200 a month. It has been over 10 years that I worked for the low salary of $1200 a month and I know John's capabilities were three or more times that - so how would John Brown have to borrow so much "cash" from you to provide such a meager living for his wife and children? Bernie, you are a "clown" and making as big a fool out of yourself as John Brown. Telling one lie to cover another. I can hardly imagine a family that Gen gave you being able to look up to you and respect you for lowering your own principles to cover up for a "John Brown." If you had only let him suffer the consequences of his misdeeds when he was a boy instead of getting him out of one scrape (jail) after another (scrape) jail, he might have learned "crime doesn't pay." So this spoiled, disgraceful man is what my grandchildren and yours are condemned to live with. The poor children still believe he is "holy and righteous" because he told them so and you have backed him 100%. And he takes them down to the front row in church to let everyone see him - the righteous one. For 17 years he has never sat with his family - always running around someplace in the building while Church is going on, I can testify to this. But it looked good on paper and to those who don't know him.*

*We will not go into the "adultery phase" again. He will never be forgiven for that - no matter where he hides. He can't hide from the Lord. And lying to get a Temple recommend, how could he!*

*If you had only tried to settle Jane and John's parting instead of "taking sides" - and done it fairly and squarely; there would have been a lot less hurt for the children's sake. But Bernie, you are such a "money hog" the only thing you could see is that Jane might get her own money back and profit from the house - her share. And since cheating is part of your life standards, you have resorted to stealing from your own granddaughter and daughter-in-law. Why did Jami take sides with her mother? Because she knew of John's lying, stealing, and cheating - she could see through him and knew the truth. While he had the other children blinded by buying them off, Bernie, with your money. Did you ever give Jane the cash sums or ask her whether she wanted them given to John? No, you didn't. Then why are you now holding her responsible for that gambling money and the other fake IOUs? You are not being truthful nor factual. Well we get punished whether in this life or the next - just remember that.*

*I am making a copy for each of your children as I am sure they do not realize all that has transpired over the years. And with John's false accusations they should know the mother's (Jane) given her life to raise her children only to have her children and her meager belongings stolen from her.*

*I feel also the Bishop and Stake President should also know the truth - so they won't be blinded by craftiness.*

*Also attached are the IOUs presumably received since 1968 when you encouraged John to move to California. The incredibility since 1968 is enough to quake the ground. It is impossible a "mother" can be tarred*

*and feathered in this day and time for being a "mother" and trying to get
her children out of the influence of Satan, but it has happened.*

*Sincerely,*
*Mrs. Adele Tucker*
[My grandmother]

# DIVORCED

The divorce itself was granted in early February 1984. Despite disagreement on the findings by the psychologists, the judge awarded custody of Brad, Jason, and Carrie to my dad. Mom got custody of me. The court ordered him to pay $250 per month in child support and alimony at the first of every month.

The court then had to split up everything my parents owned including cars, our 1976 GMC motor home, and the contents of the house. Mom offered to divide the household furnishings specifically requesting only the china, a sewing machine, an antique mirror, and a few small odds and ends. My dad's sisters took out the stained glass windows Mom had made for the home and gave them to her as guilt gifts. Among other demands, Dad requested that Mom "retain her maiden name and drop the name Brown legally in court as not to cause any more embarrassment to the Brown name."

I wished I could have changed my last name, too.

The house itself became the biggest issue of contention. The Malcolm Avenue house back in Los Angeles eventually sold for $265,000. Dad had used $80,000 of the sale to repay his father for

83

buying 2240 Hillview. Jane believed this made the Laguna house community property, and so it was therefore half hers.

Grandfather felt quite differently. The title of the Los Angeles house had been transferred to him via quitclaim to avoid liens filed by the board of equalization for the money Dad owed the state. Grandfather had never been fully reimbursed for buying 2240 Hillview and Dad had borrowed $105,767.64 from his parents including $11,000 for a "land deal in Vegas" and $14,750 to pay bookie.

"A mere sham," Grandfather apparently called my parents' fight over the house. He wanted the house and the money he was owed plus ten percent interest and $50,000 in damages claiming he and my grandmother had been unable to "freely deal with their property in the open marketplace."

Mom later discovered that a lot of the documentation had been falsified to justify the transaction on the Malcolm house. For example, Grandfather told the court he took the quitclaim because his son John owed him $140,000 for debts including the Caribbean cruise that Bernie had won and given to them as a gift. He claimed he had to say that because he could have gotten in trouble trying to keep the board of equalization from coming after the house. Paperwork related to the sale was also missing. There were so many duplicitous documents, they even created a fake down payment note to Bernie for the Malcolm house listing proceeds from the sale of Jane's house in Texas before that sale occurred so she couldn't say any of her personal money was in the Malcolm house. Grandfather testified to the veracity of the falsified paperwork under penalty of perjury:

## Deposition of Bernard Brown

Q: Do you know where the original Quitclaim deed is?

A: No

Q: When did you last see it?

A: I'm not familiar with whether a Quitclaim Deed had to go with the sale of the house into that escrow or not. It was either in that escrow at the time or it was in a folder in my desk drawer. That disappeared.

Q: So all the papers concerning the sale of the house have disappeared?

A: Yes.

Q: So. Sometime after this Quitclaim Deed was delivered to you; you actually sold the house to some third party?

A: Yes.

Q When you sold the property did you take back any interest in the property or did you retain any interest?

A I took back a second trust deed.

Q: Is that trust deed still outstanding?

A: No.

Q: So it was retired at some point?

A: Within six or nine months of the time we sold it.

Q: When you obtained legal title to the Malcolm Avenue property, do you know whether there was any mortgage against the property at that time?

A: Somewhere in the high twenties, twenty-eight, twenty-nine thousand. I don't recall.

Q: Do you remember what the value of the property was at the time?

A: I gave them credit for $140,000 when they signed the deed.

Q: Did you feel that the property had an equity interest of approx. $140,000 at the time?

A: I think that was more than the equity interest.

Q: Are you familiar with an entity known as EPA Investments?

A: That was the title the Japanese man [new owner] put the house in.

Q: Do you recall when that document was executed?

A: It says here on 11-28-79.


There were dates that seemed inconsistent:


Q: This is 1980. And the actual sale took place sometime in November of '79.

Why is it that you received the deed of trust so much later?

A: It was where he was supposed to make certain payments at certain times and when he couldn't do that, why, he gave us a second trust deed.

Q: All due and payable at one time?

A: Yes.

Q: The original trust deed appears to be in the principal sum of $116,500. Is that your recollection?

A: That's correct.

Q: And the second one appears to be in the principal sum of $140,000.

A: That's correct, that is what it says.

Q: Why the difference between the two?

A: I don't recall.

Q: When you sold the house on Malcolm Ave, did it result in capital gains tax of any kind to you?

A: No.

Q: Did you have to report the sale for tax purposes?

A: You'd have to ask my tax man.

Q: What was the actual selling price of the Malcolm street property?

A: I only have a vague figure... $266,000

Q: So apparently there was some cash that resulted from the sale; is that correct?

A: Oh, yes.

There was discussion of a quitclaim deed on March 30, 1979 and a possible appraisal before that time. A second mortgage was taken out and there were lies about the status of the house:

Q: What was the principal sum of the second mortgage?

A: I think it was $10,000 but I'm not sure.

Q: Why did you pay it off?

A: Because they were about to foreclose on the house. [THIS IS A LIE.]

Q: Do you remember who the trustee was?

A: No.

There were questions about the mortgage company which he can't remember.

Q: So the only one you are aware of was the first mortgage of approx. $29,000?

A: Yes.

My dad had hired one of the biggest, most high-powered attorneys in Orange County to annihilate my mom. At the end of all the battling in court, Mom was left with basically the clothes on her back. Eventually, the judge ruled in her favor and ordered Bernie and Gen to pay her $35,000 for her community share of the property. Bernie did not pay the full amount, offering $22,500. My mom couldn't fight them anymore so she agreed. After her lawyer was paid off, she got a check for $7000 and the Browns financed the $12,500 in payments of $576 a month until paid. She didn't see a dime until a year and a half after the divorce was final in October of 1984. There was no alimony and Dad retained custody of everyone but me.

During the divorce, Stephen R. Covey sent Mom a book he'd signed, "God bless you to know and feel His love and His great concern for and knowledge about your situation."

# RUNAWAY

In March 1983, while the divorce was being finalized, Mom and I moved to a small, depressing apartment at Moss Point on the ocean side of Laguna Beach. The church paid our rent, furnished the place, and provided groceries from Deseret Industries. While I was living with my mom on church welfare, Brad, Carrie, and Jason remained with Dad on Hillview Drive. Dad made a point of flaunting how happy they were.

I was absolutely miserable. I hated everything from the awful little apartment to the weird hard butter we got from the church food pantry. I hated being so broke we couldn't afford anything. I was fifteen and I couldn't stand my new life, so I tried to cope by going out and partying with my friends. Often, I would stay out all night with my boyfriend Tommy, who was nineteen and widely considered to be the best looking guy in Laguna Beach.

At one point, I told my mom I was going somewhere to stay at a friend's house for the weekend and I ran away to Colorado with Tommy and his friends, who were twin brothers. My mom sent the National Guard to go find me and threatened to have Tommy arrested if I didn't come home. Tommy dropped me off at the airport, where I caught the first plane back home. The guys went skiing without me.

All along, my dad knew how miserable I was and played upon it to try and get me back. His kids were his prized possessions and he wasn't about to let me slip out of his grasp so easily. He made sure I knew my brothers and sisters were getting toys and new bikes and going places and eating out all the time. It killed me, but I didn't crack. I simply partied and rebelled harder.

"Jami," he said, having gotten a hold of me one day. "I have something for you—a bank book with college savings in it."

As it turned out, my grandparents had set up a college savings account which they had recently started in lieu of Christmas and birthday gifts for us. He couldn't access the money. If he could have, he would have taken and spent everything the second he got his hands on it. He could use the funds as a ploy, though. I met Dad outside of the Wells Fargo bank on Ocean Avenue. He showed me a bankbook with just under two thousand dollars thinking the gift would entice me to come back "home" where my life would be so much easier.

I had a better plan. As soon as he handed me the bank book, I went inside the bank and took out all the money. Stephanie, one of my best friends, was miserable too, so instead of going home we decided it was high time to take a road trip.

Stephanie and I boarded the next Greyhound bus to San Diego. From there, we took another bus over the border into Mexico. We—two blond, fifteen-year-old gringas—got on a bus filled with Mexican nationals and chickens. We got off at Rosarito Beach, checked into the Rosarito Beach Hotel, and settled in for the long haul.

Almost immediately, everyone was looking for us, two missing girls from Laguna Beach. My dad's newspaper office was a few doors down and across the street on Broadway from the bus station. I did not know, but Jason had seen me board the bus with Stephanie and ran to tell my Dad. Determined to make himself look good by finding and saving me, Dad told no one.

No one else knew if we'd been abducted or run away or what had happened to us while we were drinking, sunbathing, and hanging out. I remember the staff looking at us and wondering what was going on, but never daring to ask.

We spent the next two weeks at the hotel living off my money. At night, we would push the furniture against the door because we were scared we might actually be abducted. At some point, I called my boyfriend Tommy to tell him where I was. He knew how rough things were at home and said he was really worried about where I was.

"I'm going to come get you and bring you back," he said. "You can come live with me.

He appeared in Rosarito Beach a few days later to bring us back to Laguna. Stephanie was ready to go home, so he dropped her off at her house.

I definitely wasn't.

The next thing I knew though, he was pulling up to my dad's house.

"What are you doing?" I shouted when I spotted my dad standing outside with his arms folded across his chest. "Your dad told me you ran away from your mother, not him," he said, but locking the car doors so I couldn't jump out. "He is going to take care of you."

As it turned out, he had been contacted by Dad who offered to pay him $1000 to go get me and bring me back as soon as I got in touch with him.

I couldn't believe he was doing that to me. My boyfriend, who I loved more than anything in the world, had turned on me for $1000. I was devastated. I wasn't even sixteen and was already facing the reality that everyone was going to leave me, cheat on me, and lie to me. I couldn't trust anyone. All I truly had was myself.

# THE MAGIC BAG

With my mom out of the picture, there was no buffer or anyone to tamp down my father's worst instincts. Not only didn't he care enough to try to hide what he was up to, but he dragged us into many of his questionable activities. His gambling addiction became a family affair that included taking us with him to Las Vegas and making us stay in hotel rooms by ourselves while he went out and gambled all night long.

Our house was quickly transformed into party central, complete with air hockey and arcade-sized Pac Man, Asteroids, and multiple pinball machines set up in the landing outside of my bedroom. He and the boys would stay up until two in the morning most nights of the week. I'm sure my insomnia stems, in part, from trying to drown out the pings, bonks, and weird techno music so I could sleep during those days. We'd wake up for school and ask for lunch money. He'd point to a stack of hundreds on the dresser, sometimes multiple times in a week, then he would go back to sleep while we got ourselves ready. Or not. He didn't much care either way.

The only thing Dad claimed to care about was Mom. He talked about her constantly. My friends would come over to pick me up and I'd come downstairs only to find they'd been cornered by him.

"How long have you been here?" I would ask.

"A while. Your dad's been talking about your mom."

They were so scared of my dad, who one friend described as "like a mafia godfather" in whose ramblings they felt should feign interest. He would draw in whoever was around with, "Jane did this, Jane did that…"

He really thought she wasn't going to leave him. He truly believed she was going to come back one day. Sociopaths like my dad are convinced of their own crazy reality. Even after my mom had been gone for years he would say, "I still love your mom."

*You love my mom and this is what you did to her?* I would think. *Yeah, yeah, you really must have loved our mom.*

My mother used to say, "If something wasn't tied down, John Brown would steal it."

My father was already an established kleptomaniac, so it was not entirely surprising how different his concept of grocery shopping was from hers. After dinner, which usually occurred at one of the local restaurants, Dad would pull up to our local Circle K. At that time of night, it's quiet in a beach town and very few people are out roaming the streets.

"Come on," he'd say. "We're going inside to get some stuff for the house."

What that meant was he was going to make us get out of the car in the middle of Laguna Beach, go inside, and literally rob the store. He'd paid off an employee who we only knew as *Guacamole* so he could stand by the door while we grabbed whatever food we could carry. We'd bring the stuff up to the register and Dad would say, "Go to the car. I'll take care of paying for it all."

My father always seemed to have someone he paid to do "work" for him. I definitely think he thought he was the godfather like my friends feared. There were older men, young men, even kids he kept on his own personal payroll. At the time, we called them his slaves because he would always have one around, doing what he said. Their work ranged from looking the other way (like José the Hispanic boy Dad had nicknamed Guacamole, because he'd first met him working at El Pollo Loco in Laguna), to washing his cars, running errands, picking up stuff, stealing, or going with him to be a decoy. He always needed people to accomplish things. At some point, Guacamole got kicked out of his house and Dad said he could come live with us in our Hillview house. He was so appreciative of my dad's "kindness," he pretty much did whatever my dad asked from that point on—legal or not.

We, however, had no choice.

That groceries now meant junk food, was the least terrible part of the whole situation. When dad didn't have a "buddy" who'd been paid off to allow us to shoplift freely, the stakes got higher. In other words, more fun—at least for Dad. He would stand at the register and distract the clerk with questions like, "What kind of cigarettes are those?" so he or she would have to turn around. That, or he'd ask for something in the back storage room. While the employee was otherwise occupied, we were to grab anything and everything we could get our hands on and hurry back to the car.

Sometimes he'd say, "We're going to have some fun," and pull out the *Magic Bag*—a black attaché briefcase that meant he was in a serious shoplifting mood. When I saw it come out, I knew shit was going down.

At the post office, he would reach behind the counter and grab a whole sheet of stamps. If a receptionist at an office got up to get somebody, he would look over the desk for a purse and take her wallet. He used that bag to steal anything that was both small and expensive—rolls of film, batteries, etc., which he would stockpile and lock in his office. Really valuable stuff went into the safe.

The Magic Bag made its way all over town, but certain places like the office store on Forest Avenue were his favorites. We went there all the time and he had us fill the bag with pens and all kinds of supplies. When an item was too big to fit in the Magic Bag, he'd improvise. We'd go to a golf store and he would take a club, go into the corner and slip it into his pants all the way down his leg, and walk out of the store.

I hated these trips, especially "grocery shopping" and complained bitterly. "I'm not doing this. This is crazy. I'm not going in."

"You're going to draw attention to yourself. Get out of the car right now!" he commanded in a deep, scary voice that told me I had no choice.

After a while, I wouldn't get in the car with him if I thought he was going "shopping."

Jason and Carrie were little and didn't know any better than to believe it was good clean fun to walk out with school supplies or a pile of cereal and candy for free. I witnessed it happen on numerous occasions.

I would say, "Jason and Carrie are little kids; you're making these two little kids steal stuff? That's not fun, it's sick."

He ignored me completely or punished me for being too mouthy.

Because people were always after my dad, we were constantly getting a new phone number. We didn't have cellphones back then and our home phone was usually unplugged so he wouldn't hear it ring. It was very easy for him to fly under the radar because he simply *didn't get* the calls.

When the phone was plugged in and rang, my father would make one of us answer. He'd stand right beside us while we handled the call exactly the way he'd trained us:

"Brown residence."

"Is your dad there?"

"May I ask who's calling?"

"Steve Peterson."

We'd repeat the name aloud so my dad would hear it. "Steve Peterson."

"Tell him I'll be home next week," he'd whisper while we were trying to relay the message to the person with my dad in the background feeding us whatever lie he wanted repeated.

As soon as we hung up, we'd get in trouble because we inevitably didn't say it right somehow.

"I'm not answering your phone," I would say. "I don't want to ever answer the phone again."

And then the phone would ring an hour later.

"Get the phone and do exactly as I tell you to do," he would say. "Now."

If Dad happened to spot someone pulling up to the house—often a constable or sheriff looking to serve him a warrant or a person looking for money he owed them—he would bark out a different, equally specific, set of instructions, then hide behind the door to make sure we executed them exactly as he'd told us to, complete with crazy signs and non-verbal directions.

"My dad's not here."

"Well, where is your dad? His car's out front."

"I don't know. He's not here."

"Do you know where he is?"

We were kids forced to lie to cops and scared to death we weren't saying the right thing knowing we might just get the crap beaten out of us as soon as that door shut.

We were, at once, his children, hostages, enablers, and his bodyguards.

There was a boy who lived down the street next door to our aunt. Our dad had a falling out with his father. Whenever there was a problem with a parent, my dad trained us to cause a problem with the kid or intimidate them, so this kid was in our sights.

We gave him trouble regularly.

One day, my little sister was walking home from school with a volcano project. The boy called her a moron (instead of a Mormon.) She smashed the volcano over his head and roughed him up pretty good. When Jason got wind of what happened, he took a key to the family Corvette one day in the Thurston Junior High parking lot. He keyed the entire car and went back to class.

The police came and arrested him in class. He was led out of school in handcuffs.

Jason never went to court. I can only presume his parents were threatening to press charges, so Dad must have paid them off to keep my brother out of jail. After all, Jason had learned the technique directly from my dad who was all too handy with keys and auto paint.

Just like my father, Jason clearly didn't learn from his first real brush with the law, or any of my dad's verbal assaults intended to beat the bad out of him. The two were eerily alike and they both knew it.

In all parts of his life, John Brown moved people like pawns in a chess game. He used money and his temper to get the job done. During the holidays the year I was fifteen, I went into Neiman-Marcus with a girlfriend and applied to be a gift-wrapper. I said I had a work permit. My dad found out somehow and went into the employment department and told them I was underage. No way he was allowing me to earn any of my own money and lose even a little control over me.

My brothers and sisters were smart enough to know you had to do what he wanted you to do or you wouldn't be able to go places, get new bikes, or really, anything at all. Even though I'd come back to live with him like he wanted, I wasn't about to turn into a trained monkey just to do his dirty work. I spoke up if I didn't agree. I back-talked and defied. As a result, I would always be grounded and have things taken away.

Brad pulled me aside one time and said, "Jami, your life would be so much easier if you would just do what he tells you to do and walk away. That's why you get in trouble. That's why you get things taken away. That's why all this stuff happens. Just do what he tells you to do. It's going to be so much better for you."

"I've tried, Brad. I can't. He's crazy."

"Just do it, Jami. Play the game and keep your mouth shut, so everything will be okay."

Except that nothing was okay.

# MOTHERLESS CHILDREN

Unlike my Dad, Mom was left all alone with no children to parent. Dad had made sure of that.

My grandma was living in Alaska at the time, so Mom, who couldn't afford to stay in Laguna Beach, left in June 1983, and spent the summer working in Anchorage at a printing shop. I think she wanted to get as far away from my father as possible, but it was very hurtful. My siblings had already been poisoned against her, so everything she did was further proof of how little she cared about us. Even though I wasn't living with her, I felt abandoned. Why hadn't she chosen to stay close and try to protect us? To add insult to injury and fueled by vocal speculation on my dad's part that she'd been cheating on him, Mom got remarried almost right away to a chiropractor named Kevin.

In August of 1983, they moved back to California and settled north of San Diego in Leucadia, which was still too far away. I visited her regularly. My mom made Brad a quilt to take with him when he went to college and brought it to the Hillview house. She called and met him at the back of the house. Carrie found out that he was secretly seeing Mom, and said she wanted to see Mom too. Brad took Carrie (age 13) down to see her for the first time since she'd returned from Alaska on Christmas Eve, 1983.

Mom's visitation rights had been made into such a game that she'd been forced to stop trying and it had been nearly two years. She couldn't believe her little baby girl, almost eleven, looked so grown up and so much like her.

Jason still refused to have anything to do with her.

# TIDES AND TIMES

I'll never know how or why, but somehow my dad decided to go into the local beach newspaper business, buying the *Tides and Times* in Laguna Beach, and eventually *The Beacon* in Dana Point. Both newspapers were subsequently sold to the *Orange County Register*, which became part of the *L.A. Times*. This period was the most successful of his adult life. Advertising sales funded the publication and he eventually had fifteen or twenty employees, including Wyland, who later became famous for creating numerous whaling murals throughout Southern California and the entire country.

Dad needed to be in control of everything, so running a newspaper was ideal for him. He decided what was and wasn't written, and he published the police blotter—omitting any mention of himself when he got into trouble. John Brown became prominent and well-known—a leader in the community—and often, much to our horror, used the back page to advertise our sports achievements, the family Christmas card, and whatever he wanted the community to know about his lovely, attractive, wholesome family.

Dad's office in downtown Laguna looked out onto the intersection of Cliff Drive and Broadway Avenue—perfect for him because he could see everything that was going on. He somehow always seemed to know where I was going and what I was up to. It was hard to get away with anything because he was somehow two steps ahead. When we used the car, he'd always know because he would mark the curb. He was just everywhere all the time. I learned one of his tricks one day when I was at his office and noticed the last phone line, the one with no number associated with it, blinking. I pushed the button and held the phone to my ear. My brother, who was home at the time, was on the phone with his friend. That was how I discovered that Dad had the home phone line synched up with the lines at *The Tide and Times* so he could listen in on our phone conversations and keep track of us.

Thankfully, there were benefits to his new career as well. He would do trade for advertising and soon had open accounts at many of the local restaurants. We'd eat out with our friends for free and sign the tab any time we wanted anything. All we had to do was go in and say, "We're John Brown's kids."

When he wasn't at the office, Dad was still on the golf course, gambling, and getting into trouble. Sunday was the biggest sports betting day of the week, so he'd drop us off at church, drop off his bet money, and inevitably pick us up late. He was late getting us anywhere and everywhere. I remember crying because I was late to a friend's sweet sixteen beach birthday party.

"The party won't start until you get there," he would say—yet another motto he lived by.

Narcissistic to be sure.

My dad always rode the line, especially when it came to his criminal activities. He was in and out of various jails on a regular basis. Along with the shoplifting, there were countless other mostly petty, minor offenses that continually had him on the wrong side of the law. In his book, misadventures that only cost him a minor slap on the wrist were worth doing. He got caught regularly and was in and out of the Orange County jail, but not for any truly extended length of time. If you were a prominent white guy from Laguna Beach, you maybe went to jail for a few months, never prison. They called it Camp Orange County. My dad knew he wasn't going to do hard time for his petty crimes and minor felonies and that he wouldn't be there long—a few days, a few weeks. Once, for example, he did a short stint before the holidays and was released on Christmas Eve. For all of his many faults, he always did it up big for the holidays. That year, however, everything but Thrifty (a now out of business drug store chain in California) was closed before he could shop. Undaunted, he took us and he bought all the presents there, wrapped them, and we had what would forever be known in our family as the Thrifty Christmas.

We got used to Dad getting thrown into jail but were too scared to tell anybody. Because we thought social workers would come and get us, we didn't even tell our relatives on the street. When anyone would knock on the door we would just hide in the house.

His brush-ins with the law had other unanticipated consequences as well.

One hot summer Saturday, my girlfriends and I were bored. We got on our mopeds and decided to go buy squirt machine guns. We filled the guns with water down by the beach and drove through Laguna, two on one moped and one on the other, squirting tourists as we rode by.

We stopped for lunch at Gina's pizza, hiding our scooters in the back. We got stoned, got pizza, and went back to our scooters. One of the well-known Laguna Beach motorcycle officers saw us on the top of the hill. She radioed in and we were soon surrounded by cop cars.

Somebody claimed they'd crashed their car and someone else had called in saying they'd been "blinded" by some blonde girls on mopeds spraying people with a suspicious substance. The next thing we knew, the squirt guns had been put into evidence bags and we'd been loaded into the back of the police car, three teenage girls in bikinis. We were taken into Laguna Beach police department, locked into a room monitored by the Laguna Beach patrol, and assured we were in a lot of trouble.

My dad heard this on the police scanner as it was happening. Before we even reached the station, I spotted Jason and Carrie on their BMX bikes riding alongside the police car and pointing at me. My father had told them, "Go to the police station. Jami is headed there and she's in trouble."

They escorted me all the way but couldn't do anything to help me get out.

When the police realized the whole incident had been way overblown, all the parents got a phone call to pick up their daughters. As all of my friends got picked up, I was left behind. When the police called him and said he needed to come get me, Dad said. "I don't have a daughter who would do something like that."

The real reason my dad didn't come is because he had outstanding warrants for his own arrest and couldn't show his familiar face at the Laguna Beach police department.

Eventually, my uncle came to bring me home, but I was in jail for hours longer than anyone else.

# Protective Custody

My issues with my dad continued to intensify. I did what I wanted and stayed out all night which angered him to no end. One day, I was trying to go to the beach with my friends, but Dad said, "You're grounded. You're not going anywhere!"

When I ignored him, he grabbed me, threw me to ground, held my hands down, and put his body weight on top of me to stop me from running out of the house. When I began to scream and yell in protest, he made Jason hold a pillow over my face.

"Suffocate her! Pass her out!" he repeatedly shouted.

To this day, Carrie, who saw it happen, cannot talk about the suffocation incident. If Jason had accidentally killed me, he would have been in trouble, not Dad. He would have said, "Jami was uncontrollable, she wouldn't listen to me. What choice was there?"

It was traumatizing for all of us.

One week later, on June 24, 1983, I was at his office. I was trying to get away from him and I was making a scene because he wouldn't give me the keys to my scooter, which was my only means of transportation and allowed me to get away from him on a daily basis. I wanted everybody to know he was crazy. I was screaming.

"You better lower your voice right now in front of these people," Dad said.

"I'm not going to lower my voice!"

Our fight became a full-blown physical altercation. As I was try-ing to run from him, he punched me in the face and dragged me, kicking and screaming, out to his brown Bronco which was parked in a covered underground area. He shoved me inside and handcuffed me to the steering wheel.

While I was out there, one of his employees arrived and parked close to the Bronco. She looked at me in horror, ran into my dad's office, and said, "Your daughter's out there handcuffed to the steer-ing wheel screaming her head off."

"I had to handcuff her to the steering wheel because she's so cra-zy," he told her. "She can't be controlled."

Never mind how freakish and abusive the whole thing was, did anyone wonder why John Brown just happened to have handcuffs in his car?

He then came outside and over to the Bronco, stuffed a golf towel in my mouth, and tied it around the back of my head so I couldn't scream. He stationed Carrie and Jason in a tree at the top of a nearby hill to stand guard and make sure nothing happened to me while he went back into the office to work. Undaunted, I looked in the ashtray knowing he kept spare keys in various hiding spots: on a tire, in the gas tank area, and inside the car. Sure enough I was right.

I managed to slip one of my hands free of the handcuffs, cutting my arm up pretty badly in the process. I could not move my other shoulder because it was dislocated, but I started that Bronco up and hit the gas.

As I did, Carrie and Jason ran down the hill to get Dad.

I put the Bronco in reverse and drove to Laguna Beach Police station where I held down the horn until the police came out and found me gagged and handcuffed to the steering wheel.

"My dad, John Brown, did this," I told them the second they pulled the long thin golf towel out of my mouth, which I'd left in as proof of what he had done. I knew he'd lie and say I made it up.

They went to the newspaper to find him.

"She's crazy and out of control. I had to get her calmed down," my dad said, just like I assumed he would. "I'll come and get her."

"I'm afraid we can't release her to you," they told him. "She has signs of a struggle and bruises from what appears to be a prior incident. We're taking your daughter into protective custody."

I was taken to the Albert Sitton Home for abused children in Santa Ana. I was processed, given a pair of used white tennis shoes, a white t-shirt, and jeans, and placed inside amongst seriously abused kids, including a set of twins whose hands had been put on burners. In comparison, I didn't feel like what I'd been through qualified me for a bed in that place. I guess when you are in a survival mode, nothing seems a big deal. I kept saying, "I don't belong here, I don't belong here, I want to go home." In my mind, I'd only been gagged and handcuffed and beaten. "I'm fine. I want to go back to my dad."

"You can't go back to your dad," I was told. "And in these court papers it shows that your mom beat your younger brother and sister, so we can't give you back to her, either."

"That's a lie! My mom never touched any of us!" I said, bawling my head off. "Pllleeeeaassseee! I'm begging you!"

On 6/29/83, the court gave me to my mom's sister, Aunt Jackie who lived north of Los Angeles in Westlake Village. Her husband, Uncle Carl, picked me up.

I didn't want to be at my aunt's house in the middle of nowhere. It was hot there and I wanted to be at the beach with my friends in Laguna. I just wanted familiarity. Even though it was bad at my dad's, I wanted to go back and deal with whatever happened, not live poor with my mom who'd returned from Alaska that August, or in sweltering Agoura Hills with my aunt. I just wanted to be at the beach with my friends, living my normal life.

I stayed with my aunt through the summer and then managed to make my way back to my dad's in Laguna. In September, I started my junior year at Laguna Beach High School.

**From the social worker's report of September 22, 1983:**

*The minor, Jami, age 16, was declared a dependent child of the Orange County Juvenile court under section 300(a) of the Welfare and Institutions code on August 31, 1983, as it was alleged that the minor was physically and emotionally abused by her father. Jami was taken into protective custody on June 24, 1983 by the Laguna Beach Police Department when she was involved in a fight with her father during which he struck her with his fists and stuffed a sweater in her mouth.*

*She was observed to have bruises under both eyes, a swollen shoulder, cuts inside her mouth and a painful jaw.*

*The minor also alleged that two weeks earlier, her father struck her head and shoulder then handcuffed her to the steering wheel and gagged her to silence her. A child abuse registry report had been previously filed on September 29, 1982 alleging that the minor's mother, Jane Brown had been physically abusive to the minor's siblings, Brad and Jason, while the parents were in the process of securing a divorce.*

*Progress under Supervision*
*The minor has resided with her father, David John Brown, and her two brothers Brad age 17, Jason age 14, and her sister Carrie age 12 at 2240 Hillview Drive in Laguna Beach since August 31, 1983. She continues to have various difficulties at this placement, although she appears to have adjusted to this living arrangement. The minor has been attending Laguna Beach High School and she will complete the eleventh grade in June 1984.*

*The minor has had ongoing attendance problems at her school and the family was recently referred to the School Attendance Review Board in regard to these difficulties. During the reporting period, Jami has had limited contact with her mother who has attempted visitation on a few occasions. Jami has verbalized a desire to have ongoing visitation with her mother; however, she indicated that she frequently has difficulties in her relationships with her siblings, when they become aware of Jami's contact with her mother. Attempts to comply with the stipulations concerning the visitation plan have not been successful, for a variety of reasons, including the minor cancelling visitations, the minor's siblings failing to communicate messages to Jami from her mother, ongoing bitterness in the relationship between the parents and Mrs. Brown preferring not to create additional problems for Jami at her present living arrangement. Mr. Brown has told the undersigned that visitations have not materialized as a result of the mother's lack of interest in the minor and Jami's desire not to have contact with her mother.*

*Mr. Brown was interviewed in regard to the minor on November 3, 1983 and January 6, 1984 and he advised that Jami had readjusted to living in his home in a satisfactory manner. He acknowledged some minor difficulties in Jami's relationship with her siblings; however, he attributed these problems to the minor's negative reaction to her brothers and sister. Nevertheless, the minor has been more responsive to his supervision during the reporting period. Mr. Brown informed that he was not opposed to any of his children visiting with their mother, although Mrs. Brown has never indicated an interest in having contact with her other children. He maintains that Mrs. Brown has failed to contact him during the majority of the reporting period in regard to visitation or she has cancelled visits. Mr. Brown has insisted that his ex-wife contact him over the telephone by Thursday of the same week, if she planned to visit with Jami.*

*The mother, Mrs. Brown was interviewed over the telephone on October 21, 1983, November 29, 1983, and January 19, 1984… living with her sister… in Agoura, CA. On Jan 19, 1984 she was temporarily separated from her husband… In the past six months Mrs. Brown has visited with Jami on two occasions while living in Leucadia and Agoura… Mrs. Brown stated that she has not pursued visitation more vigorously because she believes her contact with the minor creates problems with the other members of the family. She related arranging a visit on one occasion, and when she arrived at the Brown residence after driving from Leucadia, she was told Jami was not at home. Mrs. Brown also claims that the minor's siblings have hung up the telephone when she has attempted to phone Jami during the reporting period. She maintained that Mr. Brown has been responsible for influencing the children to act in this manner and has attempted to sabotage all visitation since the last Court hearing. On January 19, 1984, Mrs. Brown related that she would be able to provide a home to the minor if Jami could no longer manage in her present living environment.*

# ACTING OUT

My brother Brad did his best to follow the advice he gave me by keeping his head down and doing what he was told, objectionable though it often was. Jason became a master of penny criminality, using whatever skills he'd learned to his advantage. Carrie managed to play bystander. I, however, remained pissed off and rebellious and was by far, the wildest of all.

I wasn't accountable to anybody. I had lots of friends and was popular across high school social groups because I was an athlete, a partier, and, by my appearance, a rich girl. We lived in one of the nicest neighborhoods. I had great clothes and carried a Louis Vuitton purse I'd charged on a credit card I'd stolen from my dad. Because I didn't really have a mom around, I was wilder than anyone, and was always looking to have fun.

They called me Downtown Jami Brown.

I would stay out all night with my boyfriend or friends drinking, smoking weed, and carrying on. Anything I could do or take to numb my life and feelings was good by me.

After my stint at Albert Sitton, I was required to see a therapist by court order. My dad, who was always trying to control me, located someone in Pasadena, which was an hour and a half away (with no traffic) specifically so he could get me into the car every Wednesday afternoon and try to talk to me the whole time. I had no choice but sit beside him for the duration of what was inevitably a two plus hour drive in both directions. I thought of it as my weekly brainwashing, tag teamed by him and the joker of a shrink he'd found to "treat me" for being his difficult child.

On one particular Wednesday, I got in the car after school starving. "I want a smoothie or I'm never going to make it to Pasadena," I said.

"No problem," he said, and stopped at a snack shack on the coast of Crystal Cove called The Shake Shack. I ordered a banana date shake, paid for the drink, got back in the car, and we started on our way. I enjoyed the first sips of my drink and then some guy cut him off while we were merging back onto Pacific Coast Highway.

Dad yelled, "Give me your shake!"

"I've only had a little bit," I said.

"Now!"

"No!" I said but took another quick drink as quickly as I could, knowing what was about to happen.

He grabbed the shake from my hand. "Roll down your window."

Filled with dread and knowing he'd reach right over me if I didn't, I rolled down my window. As soon as I did, he heaved the shake right past my face into the guy's open window.

The shake sprayed all over the inside of the man's car and the startled driver began weaving all over the road.

Amazingly, the guy got off easier than some of the victims of his road rage. My dad always carried wrenches, screwdrivers, hammers, and a variety of other tools in his cars. Not in case the car broke down, but as ammunition to throw at other drivers on the road.

If somebody cut my him off or, God forbid, flipped him off, he'd pull out a wrench and throw it at their car. If he was headed down the 405 freeway and they'd start to exit, he'd pull up right next to them and throw the tool into their windshield. Dad got away with it most of the time because there weren't cell phones and he drove cars that weren't his or had switched plates.

On that particular day, my father continued on like nothing happened and we made our way to *my* psychiatrist appointment where he would sit directly outside the door and try to listen in. I could see his feet.

At first, I tried to tell the therapist what life was like with my father and that most, if not all, of my issues were because of him.

The therapist, who'd been manipulated ahead of my visits, didn't believe me. After all, my dad had already told the guy everything about me so he had a preconceived idea of my issues. I could practically hear the words in my head: *She's not listening, she doesn't obey me, she doesn't do what she's told...*

Once I realized it was my word against my dad's, and my dad was theoretically paying for the sessions, I sat silently and didn't say a word for the whole hour.

My therapy didn't last long.

# Laguna Barbie

Sometimes, my dad would wake me up in the middle of the night on a school night and say, "Get in the car."

"Why?" I'd ask, knowing it wasn't going to be an educational experience, and that whatever he had in mind either meant trouble or that I'd be missing school the next day, or both.

"Let's go," he'd say.

Sometimes we were off to repossess cars. It was an often terrifying side gig he was fond of that on at least one occasion involved an unhappy soon-to-be-former owner brandishing a gun. He always drove the repossessed car away, but we would spend hours following people and waiting for the time to "take it."

On other occasions he'd say, "Let's go," and make me get into a second car in order to follow him to San Diego and then across the border to a sports betting joint in Tijuana. He'd often have me bring whatever guy I was dating, or a guy friend to look out for me. We'd have to wait for him to do his betting and cash out. Then, he would take the panels off of the car I was driving, pack it with money, and send me back across the border. He would instruct me on what to say to the border agent if I got pulled into the secondary line.

Because it was better us than him, the word "NO," or any variation of, "I am not doing that," was not an option. He justified it by the fact that he wouldn't put more than $10,000 in the vehicle, but we were his mules who did his dirty work.

In September 1984, Brad had graduated from high school and went off to a Mormon church college, where he would spend a year before going on his mission. As the older sibling, he had done more than his share of general caretaking. Thankfully, a nice young kid named Sean started working as an errand boy at the newspaper while he was in high school. When he graduated, Sean not only stayed on doing whatever was needed down at the paper, but also looked out for me and my sister.

As a young girl, Carrie was with Sean all the time. She went and printed the newspaper with him every Wednesday evening, getting back home past midnight. Seeing as our father regularly left her alone or in the company of the various people around him, I felt secure knowing Sean was an upstanding person and would never take any kind of advantage of her.

I knew this because Sean was also good to me, taking me to the emergency room with severe stomach pain after my dad dismissed it, saying I was faking it or hung over. As it turned out, I had appendicitis but Dad wouldn't show up at the hospital because he didn't want to sign the release authorizing surgery (and obligating him to pay for the procedure). The hospital had no choice but to do the emergency surgery or I would have died from an appendix that was about to rupture.

My Aunt Sherri picked me up and brought me back home.

By mid-junior year, I'd basically stopped going to school. My dad was always out with some woman or another so I would forge my attendance notes on a regular basis. On the weekends, it was party time. I hung out with a posse of girls from Laguna and nearby Dana Hills. One afternoon, the Laguna half of our contingent piled into my best friend's white VW convertible bug with an ample supply of wine coolers and picked up the Dana girls. On the way home from our wild day in Mission Viejo, we saw an open back gate for Ben Brown's golf course and decided to take a shortcut through, saving us fifteen minutes. Drunk, it made perfect sense to us to drive a convertible directly across the golf course. We ended up being chased by multiple people in golf carts as others shot balls at the car and warnings blared over the loudspeaker.

Somehow, we got across the course and escaped without being caught.

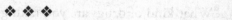

For my sixteenth birthday, Dad presented me with a Rolex, in the box, complete with diamond bezel. Where or how he'd gotten it, and why he'd given it to me instead of one of his lady friends was anyone's guess. It was definitely not something I should have been wearing around. One night, around one in the morning, my friends and I decided we needed to have a *recreational experience*. We drove to the canyon to the friendly neighborhood dealer everyone knew about. He was more than happy to oblige our little party-hearty group of underaged blondes. The only issue was that we didn't have enough cash between us and needed to bring him the rest later.

"What do you have for collateral?" he asked.

I slipped that Rolex right off my wrist.

Unfortunately, the drug dealer got busted along with the IOU log he kept. My name was written inside: *Jami Brown. Rolex watch. Owes $350.*

My dad got a call from the police to let them know I was a client and that they had the watch. I always had to check in when I came home after midnight. On this particular night, Dad sensed I was on something, so instead of letting me go, he instructed me to sit in the chair in the corner where a bright light shone above my head. He was sitting up in his bed but I could only see him as a shadow in the dark.

Weirdly, I was never punished. Instead, he, who didn't drink or do drugs at all, seemed to be more curious than anything. He wanted to understand and interrogated me at length.

"Why are you doing drugs?"

"How do they you make feel?"

"What kind of drugs are you taking?"

I was already on a path of no return, so I just let it all out and told him everything. I figured there was nothing he could do to stop me. There was only one thing I couldn't say, although it was the most important truth of all: *I like drugs because they numb me out so I can escape from you.*

I do believe he was starting to understand that things had gotten crazy beyond control. The next time he caught me skipping school, he reported me for truancy and had me taken to juvenile hall, the plan being to scare me straight. I was processed, given a dingy gray jail uniform and socks, and put into solitary confinement for *my own protection*. As a mere truant, I was deemed to be at risk amongst the general population.

It was right before Christmas and I spent two days by myself in a cell with no windows. I remember volunteers coming in and singing Christmas carols. It was creepy, horrible, and not at all festive. My dad came to visit me with Jason and Carrie. I thought he was coming to get me out, and apparently, he could have. I later learned he told my siblings, "I am going to leave her in there for a few more days to teach her a lesson."

He finally came to get me on Christmas Eve—getting out of jail having become something of a family holiday tradition.

Despite my jail stint, I partied my way through the rest of the school year. On the weekends, we were was usually in our bikinis hanging out at a certain spot at Victoria/Lagunita Beach. The summer I was sixteen, a well-known professional athlete owned a beach house there. While his beautiful, blond wife always hung out on the deck of their home, he and a friend who was also a famous athlete, were often down by the water. One day, they came over, introduced themselves, and stuck around and chatted with us. The athlete's teenage son happened to be out on a jet ski.

"I'm going to go meet him," I said.

"Right," everyone said, thinking I was kidding.

I got up, dove into the waves, swam out to him, said hello, and he invited me onto the jet ski for a ride.

We all made pals with the boy. One evening we invited him to go get sushi with us at one of the local restaurants where I had a tab. We lied about our age and they served us alcohol without carding us. Dad got a big bill, which I got into a lot of trouble for later. That night, the athlete's son nearly passed out. We drove him home but didn't know what to do with him. We didn't want to leave him there, out cold on the front steps, so it was decided that since I was the brave one, I had to let his father know he was home. We all dragged him to the doorway together. The other girls scurried back to the car and I rang the doorbell.

When the famous athlete answered, I said, "Thanks!" and took off.

That was the last time we saw either of them. It was probably a good thing, seeing as the athlete and his family would soon become even more infamous than mine.

# TOP OF THE WORLD

"If you don't come home tonight, I'm kicking you out of the house," Dad said in early March 1985, part way through my senior year. "I mean it this time."

*Yeah, whatever,* I thought knowing he probably wouldn't even be around when I got home anyway. He was dating a woman named Donna and would probably be at her place if the impulse came upon him to act like something resembling a parent.

"All your stuff is going to be outside," he said as I took off.

After yet another night of partying, I rolled in at around 6:00 AM. I snuck down the back stairs to my room and discovered my key wouldn't work in the lock. Not only had he actually gone and locked me out, but all of my belongings were outside on the patio—including my bed and my clothes.

Bleary and not knowing what else to do, I crawled into the bed and went to sleep on the patio.

I awoke to blazing sunlight and my dad standing over me.

"You can't live here anymore," he said. "You're uncontrollable."

I later discovered that he cancelled my California driver's license as additional punishment.

I walked around the corner to my aunt's house and told her I'd been kicked out and that all my things were on the patio.

"Come on in," she said.

It was one of the many times I was hugely grateful to have extended family so close by.

From that point on, I lived with my aunt, ignoring my dad every time I drove my scooter past his house to hers. During this time, Dad, role model that he was, had to do yet another short stint in jail.

Grandfather finally had enough and made him move out of the house after he was released. Or, maybe the reason was more financial. Later, one of my uncles said the new owner of Hillview asked him why the house was mortgaged to the hilt when he bought it. Grandfather had apparently taken out quite a few loans against the house, telling everyone it was to pay off John's gambling debts. Who knows what the money was really used for?

Dad rented another house in an area ironically known as Top of the World.

I went by occasionally and was there one day when the sheriff appeared at the door.

"Hide," my father said, and jumped the back fence of the property.

It certainly wasn't the first time, and we all knew the drill, so Jason, Carrie, and I piled into different closets and covered ourselves in laundry. The sheriff came in and found all of us in our separate hiding spots.

"You're being evicted," the sheriff said. "Grab what you can and get out of here."

We did as we were told, taking everything we could and piled it onto the driveway.

My dad moved with Jason and Carrie into what was basically a shack in an area of Laguna known as the Canyon. Grandfather owned land there with a car lot where he kept the junkers he was fixing up. Located on the property was a barely habitable old house with dirt floors, a kitchenette, and a rusty refrigerator. It is now a vintage Jeep dealership.

Jason and Carrie rode their bikes out of the canyon every night to fold and deliver newspapers at the *Tides and Times*. My dad would take the shell off the Bronco on summer Saturdays, put Jason and Carrie in the back, and have them throw papers into everyone's yards.

My dad thought nothing of staying at his girlfriend's house and leaving Jason and Carrie, fifteen and thirteen, to fend for themselves. They had to get themselves up for school and came home to nothing but each other. Carrie rode her BMX bike everywhere—twice to meet Dad at his girlfriend's house, twenty miles away in Mission Viejo.

They had to take care of themselves but managed to figure things out best they could. Because they both worked for Dad and the *Tides and Times* was his business, they would take his keys off the table, go clean out the multiple newsstands, and take all the quarters out of machines when they needed money. This happened regularly, especially when dad was in jail.

Unfortunately, Jason's predilection for stealing served him well during this period of time. One day, Jason was headed to the Boys Club in Laguna and stopped along the way at the supermarket. He had his gym bag with him for basketball practice, so he stole a bunch of food from the store and shoved it into the bag. Without my father to oversee his illegal activities, he got caught. The store took pity on him and didn't call the police. Instead, they called my dad, who pretended to be horrified and got him out of there.

When he was younger, Dad had tried to beat the bad out of him. Now, he was only mad that Jason hadn't gotten away with the theft. His lack of concern had to have encouraged Jason's next bigger incident.

Jason was riding his bike down Forest Avenue one afternoon and walked into Bushard's Pharmacy to get some candy. The employees were counting the money in the register and putting it in a bag on a counter right near the candy. The second their eyes were off the money, Jason seized the moment and that bag of money. He ran out the back door, jumped on his bike, and took off.

He got caught with the money and was arrested.

Luckily for him, the amount he'd stolen was under the limit to charge him with a felony.

In true Brown fashion, he slipped by with a misdemeanor that would come off his record when he was no longer a minor.

# HIGH SCHOOL

I lived with my aunt through the second half of my senior year of high school. I behaved better while living in her home, but I still got into too much trouble. I had parties at her house and I stole her credit card which I used to rent a limo and buy alcohol. I still wonder what I was thinking, racking up a $1000 bill knowing she would see the bill. I did get a job at a local gift shop on Forest Avenue to try and pay back the money, but basically, I was still out of control.

My aunt and a host of other people did what they could to look out for me. At school, the Dean of Students did her best to keep me out of trouble and push me through high school. She caught me getting high at prom and simply said, "Be in my office first thing Monday morning."

I showed up, on time, and we had a long talk where I was as honest with her as I was with anyone. I didn't even try to hide my partying at prom. Instead of suspending or expelling me, she decided I had to meet with her every morning at 7:00 AM before school until graduation. She also planned to check in to see that I was in my classes. It was a hassle, but it meant a lot to know she was worried about me. At the end of the conversation she said, "We're not going to tell your father."

She knew that would be the worst punishment possible.

The varsity tennis coach was always doing what he could for me too. I'd get kicked off the team for having too many absences and he'd let me back on. Both of them made repeated exceptions for me because they knew my home life was nuts and they wanted to help me steer clear of John Brown. Despite all the breaks in my direction, and the fact I was smart—so smart I'd skipped a grade early on—I'd missed far too much school and hadn't cared about my grades. By the end of senior year, I was short twelve credits and couldn't possibly get my high school diploma in June 1985 with my class.

The Dean of Students said I could walk in the ceremony, but I wouldn't be graduating.

I reacted to the news by partying all night and skipping the event completely.

Dad showed up at the high school with Jason and Carrie to see me walk across the stage and I simply wasn't there.

# TRY, TRY, AGAIN

Even though my father had systematically undermined my education by using us for cover whenever he felt like it, I've always been smart and driven enough to do what needed to be done. I wasn't going to be a high school dropout. It just wasn't who I was, and I knew I had to pull it together.

My aunt was understandably fed up with me, especially since I hadn't graduated. I wasn't about to go live with my dad again, so I went to stay with my mom and her husband in Leucadia. They were living in Valley of Dreams, an upscale mobile home park a few steps from the ocean. It was small, but my mom had it decorated nicely with family photos, so it resembled something like home, just smaller. Thank goodness Mom was there to help me pick up the pieces of my broken life and get me back on my feet.

I got my first waitressing job at Paradise Cove café in Leucadia and she helped me enroll at Palomar Junior College. She also dropped me off and picked me up from class every day. In order to get my GED, I needed to take and pass five classes. Even though I was told it was nearly impossible, especially given my grades in the past, I enrolled in everything I needed and got down to it. I always had a good work ethic and was determined to get the job done.

I spent the summer working and studying. Not one to pass a spare minute lonely, I met a guy while I was out riding my bike—my only refuge from my mom's small house besides the beach. He asked me out by sending a hundred pink roses. I was seventeen and he was thirty. I wasn't in love, but he wined, dined, and drove me around in his Porsche, so I wasn't complaining.

While I was living with my mom, Dad took Jason to a baseball game at Dodger Stadium. As they were leaving, some guys decided to yell something at them. Dad, being Dad, decided to not only follow them, but had Jason help him pelt the car with a bag of bolts. He also smashed the windshield with a wrench.

Dad was caught that time and sentenced to three months in jail.

While he was doing his time, Brad, who was home from college for the summer, got the notification that Dad's storage unit payment was due. Rather than the have the storage people take the stuff, Brad cleaned it out and brought everything back to the canyon house. Angry at our father for leaving Jason and Carrie alone in a house with dirt floors to fend for themselves, and also in need of money, he blew up Dad's safe and took what they needed. Brad then loaded up some of the contents of the storage unit, including furniture from the Hillview house he believed was rightfully Mom's from the divorce. More important, he arranged for Jason (who still would have nothing to do with Mom) to live at Aunt Brooke's and packed fourteen-year-old Carrie into the car along with the furniture and brought her down to Leucadia.

Rightfully scared to death of my dad, Brad then high-tailed it to Arizona to Mom's other sister's to hide and work until it was safe to come back. After all, no one stole from John Brown.

Later, Grandfather asked Brad why he took the furniture to his mother.

"I thought when you got divorced everything was 50/50 but my mother got nothing," Brad said.

Grandfather did not reply.

Jason went to Aunt Brooke's who did her utmost to be the perfect Mormon wife and maintain the family facade. She had a great house, lots of money, and pretty clothes for her kids. For the first time since he was little, Jason had home-cooked meals, family dinners with his four cousins, and the semblance of a normal life. In his mind, Brooke was like a mother he never had.

There was no telling him anything else by that point. Mom was evil and that was that.

While he was living at Aunt Brooke's, he drove Dad's Bronco, crashing it twice. He also decided to play a joke on the maid, asking her to play Fifty-Two-Card-Pick-Up and then making her clean up the cards he sprayed around the room as the punchline of the game. She was furious, and so was Aunt Brooke, who sent him to Aunt Sherri's in December 1985.

While he was living at Aunt Sherri's, Jason made a mistake that would come back to haunt him years later. Sherri's oldest daughter was getting married and gifts were continually arriving at the house.

One day, he loaded up the Bronco with some of the wedding presents. He took them to John's apartment and stashed them in the attic crawlspace, never to be seen, at least by anyone in our family, again. I think he planned to use the items at some point, but he never came back for them. Our cousin never forgave him or forgot, especially years later when she got a call from the FBI inquiring as to his whereabouts.

While the time he spent with our aunts may have been amongst his most stable, it did little to change his overall trajectory. Particularly because he would eventually end up back at Dad's.

I ignored all the family drama that summer and studied my brains out, passing everything, and earning enough credits to get my diploma. My mom drove up to Laguna, took my transcripts to Laguna Beach High School, and met with a counselor so I could graduate and apply for college in Hawaii. She also met with our bishop to get the okay for me to do community service and set up a plan to pay Aunt Brooke some of the money I'd stolen from her on her credit card. Aunt Brooke was impressed by my diligence and helped me fill out and submit my college application.

I got into BYU Hawaii and was able to enroll for the Fall 1985 semester. Because of the help of my tennis coach, I also got a partial athletic scholarship.

I'd like to say that I changed, or at least grew out of some of my bad habits as a result my big accomplishment, but I still had a long way to go. For example, my boyfriend had to go out of town and left me the keys to his house so I could get some things I needed to pack for school. Inside the house were the spare keys to his Porsche, which I took out for a spin. And by a spin, I mean I drove up to Laguna to see some friends and crashed the car. It could still be driven, so I took it back to his house, parked it, and left a note telling him I was sorry.

Before he returned, I'd packed up all my worldly belongings and taken off for Hawaii.

# Aloha

BYU Hawaii is located forty minutes from the famous North Shore of Oahu where surfing life, big waves, and fun are the order of the day. I got to school and enrolled in my general education classes with a plan to major in psychology. I quickly discovered that even though the college was located near the fabled surfing mecca, the school was, as I call it, *Molly Mormon* central.

In other words, there were rules, rules, and more rules.

Shorts had to hit right above the knee. You could not wear sleeveless shirts or tank tops. If you wore a two-piece bikini on the beach someone would tell on you and you'd get a violation. If you got three violations, you were expelled, and there were always "narcs" ready to run and tell on you for anything and everything.

While I knew right from wrong and had plenty of examples of how I was supposed to act from my years in the Mormon church, I was completely sick of having the message hammered into my head. Growing up Mormon meant being controlled—I had to go to church, I had to behave a certain way, eat a certain way, dress appropriately. I was finally on my own and no one was going to tell me what to do. I had a hard time following rules, much less making it to class with the beach right there, cute boys all around, and good times to be had. Needless to say, I got well over three violations, but I was allowed a lot of wiggle room because I was on the tennis team.

Drinking was strictly prohibited, but there were plenty of kids who did it anyway. One of my good friends was a girl named Laura from the East Coast. She liked to drink and hitchhike around the island, often in a bikini, like I did. Laura, like most of the kids in the gang I befriended, partied and got in a bit of trouble here or there, and then found their way. I, on the other hand, was desperate for love and attention and I was determined to chart my own course amongst a well-worn path of rebellious Mormon kids. I quickly became a whole lot more interested in drinking (seeing as the legal age was 18), winning beach bikini contests, and refusing to follow the dress code than I was living on a campus filled with restrictions.

Quiet and life are two words that didn't go together in my world, but I was street smart. It was more than could be said about some of the kids around me. Early in the year, a car filled with guys drove up and offered one of the more innocent girls, fresh off a potato farm, a ride to go clubbing. She got right in. When we heard she'd gotten into a car with some random guys who definitely weren't from the school, we knew she was in trouble. A bunch of us raced down to Waikiki and went up and down the streets asking bouncers if they'd seen her. Someone recognized her as having left a place called the Pink Cadillac. We kept searching for her until someone spotted one of the guys she'd taken off with. We called the police who found her, but not until after she'd been beaten and raped.

She left school soon after.

Unwilling to live restricted in the dorms with a bunch of kids who were too innocent to know which way was up, I rented a room in a house on the Northshore with these surfer dudes from Brazil (and California) and got a salt water rusty car for $1,000 to drive back and forth to school. I liked living there. The guys were like brothers to me, a Haole girl hanging out on the North Shore of Oahu. Even though I put my dresser against the door at night because they'd get drunk and try to crawl into bed with me on occasion, they took good care of me. They went spearfishing on the beach and cooked whatever they caught for me. We spent many evenings getting stoned and eating soy sauce popcorn.

I started dating an older Mormon guy named Dan who was at BYU on the extended plan. I went to class just enough to stay on the tennis team, but I was super mouthy to the coach and was forever sentenced to running up and down the courts after practice until the sun went down.

One day, I'd had enough and told her to f... off.

She kicked me off the team.

The men's coach, another helper along the way, found out and let me practice with the men's team. It seemed like there was always someone out there trying to help me, but I wasn't willing to help myself. When the car inevitably broke down, I just quit going to school entirely.

I was expelled before the end of my second year of college.

All the while, Grandfather was sending me a monthly $1,000 room and board check to help defray my expenses. I didn't tell him I'd been kicked out and kept getting the money. I also found a live-in nannying job and figured I would settle into a quiet island life sneaking Dan (and few other guys) into the house and getting them out while the family was making pancakes in the morning.

Dan and I were dating casually but got serious just in time for him to graduate and move away. With him gone, I was left heartbroken on a too-small island with no future.

By that time, Mom was living back in Texas nursing deep wounds of her own—her husband, the chiropractor, had just left her and moved back to San Diego.

"Why don't you come here," she said. "At least we can cry together."

I was nineteen, I'd failed out of college, and I had no idea what I was going with the rest of my life, so I got a ticket and headed to Texas.

# New Digs

After I left for college, Carrie stayed at my mom's for the 1985-1986 school year. It wasn't easy for her socially, but she lettered as a freshman in tennis, basketball, and softball. Dad was less than thrilled with her decision, but she visited him and he took her on more than one ski trip to Brian Head, Utah along with various combinations of people, including Jason, his assistant Sean, and Donna.

Before the season started, Dad stole a number of ski passes so they could actually ski on the trip, as well as three pairs of skis and two pairs of boots. On the way to a winter 1986 trip, they stopped in Las Vegas at 4:00 AM so Dad could win some money and were at the slopes when they opened at 8:00 AM. He instructed Sean to sell extra passes he'd stolen to people waiting at the ticket window line. The next day, Jason and Sean were coming back from the slopes and Dad, who hadn't skied that day, was in the parking lot having been pulled over by the police. In his car were one of the new pairs of stolen skis.

Dad got arrested once again.

I know that Carrie was disgusted by the idea that her 42-year-old father was stealing stuff and didn't visit him again until late spring.

While I was away, Brad got his mission call. He was to begin in the summer of 1986 and would serve his mission in United States. In the meantime, he was back and forth between Mom's and my aunt's in Arizona, where he was earning money by helping to build Arby's restaurants for our uncle.

A month before he left, he was informed that Grandfather had no money to send him on his mission. Even though he didn't know whether the lack of funding was a punishment for his recent loyalty to Mom, he came back to Leucadia to live with her while he prepared to go.

That summer my mom and stepfather moved to Texas and Carrie decided to go with them. Carrie liked having Mom around; she had appreciated the home cooked meals, laundry, ironing, and even how Mom nagged her to stand up straight. When Carrie experienced hot humid Texas in July however, she went down to a payphone, called Dad, and said, "Get me out of here."

Dad bought her a ticket and brought her back to California within days. Given he'd never wanted Carrie to live with Mom in the first place, he was delighted. In summer 1986, Dad, who had purchased the *Beacon* newspaper in Dana Point, got an apartment in the area, behind the library and between the Ritz-Carlton and the Monarch Beach golf course.

At the end of summer, Carrie went back to Laguna Beach High School for tenth grade. Jason who had been living with Dad, entered his senior year. Even though they lived with him in Dana Point, they used Aunt Sherri's address and forged Dad's signature on all the paperwork—a no brainer given her version of his signature was the one on file at the school.

Before she moved down to Mom's, Jason and Carrie had been basically inseparable. When they were reunited back in Dana Point however, Jason was mad at her for living with Mom for so long and they weren't as close as they'd been. Still, they shared a small bedroom and spent a lot of time together.

Jason got a Volkswagen Rabbit from Dad (which would eventually be confiscated by its rightful owner who believed Dad was selling it for him) and Carrie inherited his scooter. At some point, she had a minor accident and crashed the front end. Jason and Carrie went over to the library in Dana Point by their apartment. There was a red scooter parked there. Jason stole it, put it in the back of the Bronco, brought it back to the apartment, and carried it upstairs where he took it apart and used all the parts to fix Carrie's scooter. Then, he went and dumped the stripped moped on a nearby hill. The whole event was an eerie foreshadowing of the bike Jason would allegedly dump in the bushes many years later in commission of an even bigger crime.

Carrie had grown to hate the criminality around her, not to mention the benign and not-so-benign neglect. Dad wasn't home very often and usually slept at Donna's unless they were fighting. Carrie and Jason mainly took care of themselves knowing John wouldn't be around necessarily and expecting him to pick them up late or not at all when they needed rides. When Jason missed school, Carrie would forge a note for him. While Carrie liked the freedom, she began suffering from stress headaches.

They went to church some of the time. They attended seminary more regularly because my uncle taught seminary class. Carrie's friends were all nice kids. Jason's friends, although from the church, were a bit rowdier. In the Brown family, there were twenty-seven cousins, so everyone always had a cousin/friend their own age.

Carrie was in tenth grade when she walked in on Jason and a bunch of buddies with alcohol all over the kitchen table. She was in such shock, she just went to her bedroom and shut the door.

In mid-January, Dad didn't come home when he was supposed to. Neither Carrie nor Jason were too worried, it had happened before, and, of course, he eventually showed up. Two nights later, he called Jason and Carrie into the living room for a talk. He told them someone had, "done something to him" and that he had to go to jail for fifty-seven days as a result. He would get out March 12 and to contact Donna for money.

The next morning he was gone. He'd left $50 for each of them.

Dad called from jail from time to time, but Jason and Carrie were otherwise on their own. Carrie called Donna to tell her she got a haircut for $12 and had only had $6 left. Donna told her that was too bad because Dad had arranged for them to each have $25 dollars a week, nothing more. Carrie had to depend on Jason to give her rides. If he was busy or didn't feel like it, she had no choice but take the bus. Getting to places like driver's ed, which she needed to complete to get her license, were all but impossible. When Donna ran out of the money Dad had left for my brother and sister, Grandfather stepped in, giving each of them $5 per week. Carrie remembers eating mayonnaise sandwiches or anything they could scrape together (or Jason could steal) and being unable to afford to do laundry in the coin operated machines in their apartment complex.

Carrie woke up one night to Dad entering the room. He'd gotten out early claiming some sort of technicality. Apparently, he'd actually been released on Saturday but had spent the weekend at Donna's before coming home to check in on his kids. Carrie was too glad to have the lunch money he gave her for the day to be as furious as she had every right to be.

Out of jail, Dad rented a different apartment, but little else changed. He was still rarely home. He'd come over and give Carrie and Jason money, or they'd go to him when they needed cash. They looked forward to last minute jaunts to Las Vegas with Dad, where they would go onto the casino floor knowing he'd give them a couple hundred dollars to go away before he got kicked out. They'd pocket the money and come back an hour or two later saying they'd spent it and he'd give them some more. On a good trip to Vegas they might accumulate $600 to hide under their mattress and live off for the next few months.

Donna wanted to get married—the one line Dad wouldn't cross. His M.O. was to string women along, even getting engaged and presenting them with a big rock to wear around, but he'd always dump them at the last minute with the same excuse.

"I have to take care of my kids," he'd say.

Oh, the irony.

In truth, he'd already started phasing Donna out while he charmed another woman named Nadia whom he wined, dined, and showered with gifts. Ignoring Jason and Carrie, he slept at one or another of the women's places for three straight weeks, even buying presents for Nadia's daughter. Finally, Jason called Dad and told him to come home, that they were sick of his shit.

Dad swore he'd be a better father. Whether he was or wasn't is open to interpretation.

With summer approaching, Jason came home from school, walked up the stairs and spotted Donna hiding by the door. She'd been calling for a couple of weeks, leaving messages on the machine a few with threats like, "John, if I don't hear from you in four hours, I'm calling Grandfather."

Dad wasn't calling her back.

Where's your dad?" she asked.

"I have no idea," Jason said. He assumed by the look on Donna's face that he'd broken up with her. Jason knew for sure when he opened the door to his house and Donna pushed her way inside claiming she needed to use the bathroom, but then clacked down the hallway in her high heels to nose around.

"Donna, just leave," Jason said, knowing Dad already had pictures of Nadia on his dresser.

"No," Donna said. "I'm not leaving until your father gets home."

Jason took her purse and put it outside, and then took Donna by the arm and began to pull her out of the apartment. Donna stopped and held onto the green chair and began to cry. "He told me he couldn't marry me. He said it had to end it because he needed to be there for his kids."

"Did he, now?" Jason said.

Donna wouldn't budge, so Jason had no choice but physically lift her up, getting kicked by her high heels as he removed the woman from the house. He dropped Donna on the doorstep, shut the door, and Jason left to go do homework at a friend's house.

There was nothing more they could do.

Dad wrote letters to Donna, one of which left Carrie furious, and fanned the building flames resentment she had for our father. The Dear John letter he wrote Donna when he broke up with her for good couldn't be a better example of his narcissism, lies, and obsessions with his version of the truth:

*November 26, 1986*
*Dear Donna,*
*Hi Honey—I'm sorry the way things turned out, I love you but am not in the position to get married—right now—I know how important it is to you—and the ultimatum you gave me—"either get married or we can't go on," I understand.*
*Your feeling of Jason and Carrie are very accurate—Jason is going to be ok but it will take time.*

Carrie is just as you figured—using me to the hilt and taking advantage of me all the time—she really doesn't care about me at all—she seems to exude happiness at other people's unhappiness—It's a shame the way she's treating me but maybe someday she won't have a father—I'm doing what I should—providing a home for her—loving her and making it as easy as possible on her—I'm happy that she loves her mother but everything that happens here with me or my family… she goes directly to her mother—I hope someday she can love both sides—If not she will be a very unhappy girl—

I never ask her about her mother or anything about her—it does not matter any more—But if she persists in acting the way you said she would and she certainly is—then I feel there is not much I can do for her. She certainly is not appreciative of anything I do for her—I buy her clothes—make sure she has money in her pocket but she is just using me to the hilt.

I really feel sorry for her—

Jason realizes that no matter what happens he has a strong family support system betting on him—"The Browns"—On Jane's side of the family they never have that and never will.

Brad took advantage of everyone and used them to the hilt—

Even when Jane and I got married, the Browns paid for the wedding "all of it" Jane's mother never paid a penny and the women's parents are responsible for paying for their daughter's wedding—we had a reception in L.A.—we could not have one in Houston. No one would have come and Jane said she would have been too embarrassed to have one so we didn't—How clear the picture becomes—she will never be truly happy because she is not a giving person—Remember when we discussed about her being a "Bag Lady" it's so true. I'm afraid Jami is one too. Carrie may not be—I sure hope so—For her sake. A lot of women carry that bag on *their shoulder and fill it up with negative things... and when it gets fun or they feel they have had enough, they bail out—That's what she did.*

*I must admit I feel bad—I have a chance to marry too—But my responsibility is to be with and provide for these two children. Yes— even though Carrie is using me—taking advantage of me and telling her mother everything and being devious—After all that I am doing the right thing. If she does not appreciate it, it is her misfortune.*

*Brad for all that he has done—for stealing from everyone and stealing my safe—well, he got his inheritance and ended up with a mother—he will probably never have a father—he has caused too much pain.*

*Jami put me through more here than any father should have to go thru—many, many people have told me I did more and took more from that child than anyone could ever have—so she has a mother and a dad she will probably never have—*

*Jason will make it—unfortunately he will never have a mother— what a shame—she really dumped on him—she could have been the strong one—the one to support him no matter how tough it was—She should always have been there—she will be sorry for that some day—*

*Carrie might just blow it—She had better learn to keep my life and Jane's life separate and not use one against the other—There will be a lot of unhappiness if she does not learn that –I'm truly sorry for the way Carrie has treated you—Not only was I embarrassed—I was ashamed— Please forgive her—*

*Children don't understand certain things—Here Carrie is "using me" and abusing me and someday when she goes to college and gets financing here because that may be all she gets— Because it really hurts to be put down by her—and I feel that she really does not care about me—But I am doing what's right and that's the important thing—*

*I did not dump on them like their mom did...She could care less about her kids... And until she takes care of her problem—no one will stick it out with her...*

*You are the most loving, giving and honest person their ever could be—I could be forever happy with you but I have to move out to provide a home for my children. If it were not for that we would be married.*
*Now*

*I love you——*

*John*

# CURVE BALL

On my way from Hawaii to join my mom in Houston, I met a girl on the airplane named Diane. She was pretty, blonde, the same age as me, and we made friends instantly.

"Let's go out to some clubs or whatever," she said.

For my first few months in Houston, we did just that, going out all the time. One fateful evening, Diane and I were out at bar and found ourselves staring at the same guy. He was 6'4", dark-haired and muscular, with movie star good looks. He was also glancing in our direction.

"Look at that guy," Diane said.

"I see him," I said.

"I'm going to talk to him," she said.

"No, because I'm going to get to him first," I said, and went straight over and introduced myself.

His name was Luke and he played farm ball for the Atlanta Braves. He also had a successful landscaping company. He was separated from his wife who happened to be a Dallas Cowboys cheerleader. He was twenty-nine, ten years older than me, so I told him I was twenty-one, just like my fake ID said.

We spent every waking minute together for the next week. Within two weeks, I'd moved into his huge house on Clear Lake outside of

Houston, a few doors down from Buzz Aldrin. Luke's best friend lived with him. His best friend's girlfriend was a flight attendant for Continental Airlines. She mentioned there was a huge open interview for flight attendants at the airport and that I should apply. Although it turned out there were over a thousand applicants, I'd already become someone who did everything big. As the child of a narcissistic sociopath who'd already embarked on a path of getting involved with men like my father, I'd taken on a tough, brazen confidence and self-assuredness.

In other words, I applied and was one of five people offered a job.

My mom was happy about my career path but was beyond worried about my relationship with Luke. She noted there were always liquor bottles in the trash can and thought Luke might be alcoholic. I ignored her because even though he liked to party, and although he had just flipped his BMW on the highway and gotten a DUI right before we'd met, clearly, he could handle it all. Besides, he took really good care of me, even buying me a brand-new red VW Rabbit convertible.

Also, we were madly in love.

When he asked me to marry him, it didn't bother me that we had to wait a year until his divorce was final from the Dallas Cowboy cheerleader. It seemed romantic when he insisted I get a red and black tattoo heart with a ribbon that had his name on it, especially since he got a matching one that said *Jami*. I was madly in love, had a great job traveling all over, and, for the first time, I felt free from some of the pain I'd carried around from my turbulent childhood.

When Luke agreed to be baptized in the church, my mom was happy, too.

Overlooking the fact that he'd already been married twice—first to his high school sweetheart (the homecoming queen), and that we had a justice of the peace perform the ceremony so his recent ex-wife (who was calling all the time trying to get him back) wouldn't freak out, I became gorgeous, successful, Luke's third wife in March 1988. It was one year after we met.

Growing up Mormon meant that getting married young and quickly, made perfect sense to me. I knew my life wouldn't be that of a typical Mormon girl, but it would be the *Jami* version of the same thing. I was elated to be a newlywed.

A few months into my job and my new marriage, I wasn't flying nearly as high.

Luke quickly revealed a controlling and jealous side. When he was sober, he was wonderful, but he drank even more frequently than Mom suspected. When he drank, his personality changed. If another guy touched my arm when we went out, he wanted to beat him up. He was big and threatening and would get into fights regularly.

He got physical and sexually aggressive with me, too. All the doors in his huge house had deadbolt locks on the inside. One night, he flew into a rage, pulled out all the phone cords, and locked me in the house. I couldn't get out or talk to anyone for nearly two days.

My job quickly became an escape from our tumultuous relationship. My hub was on the East Coast and I shared an apartment with a bunch of other flight attendants in Reston, Virginia, which gave me reason to get away. Three months into our new, troubled marriage, however, I began throwing up during takeoffs, landings, and sometimes even during the flight.

I was, of course, pregnant.

Six months into my new career, I had to take a leave of absence.

While I was thrilled I was going to be a mother, my relationship with Luke continued to degrade. He would pick a fight with me, storm out of the house, and be gone all night long. I didn't know where he was going, or where he'd been because he would lie. He would just say he was out driving his truck. One night, I got in my car and started driving down the main highways in our area to go find him myself. I was shocked and horrified to spot his truck parked in a strip club parking lot. I was as wild as they came for a Mormon girl, but I'd never been to such a place and couldn't begin to imagine why Luke was there.

Which didn't stop me from marching directly inside.

I spotted him seated at a table drinking his Chivas and water and staring up at the dancers. I went right up to him, pulled his gold necklace off his neck, and started beating on him.

A bouncer grabbed me and threw me out.

Even though I was pregnant, Luke did nothing to stop him.

I called my dad, heartbroken and sobbing, to tell him everything that had been going on.

"I'm on my way," he said.

Less than twenty-four hours later, Dad and Jason showed up from California driving a U-Haul. No strangers to stealth missions, they lurked outside until Luke went to work. As soon as he was gone, they put me on a plane back to Orange County. Then, in true fashion, the two of them emptied the house of nearly everything and headed back to California. Luke, who'd never even explained why he thought it was okay to leave his pregnant wife at home while he went to a strip club, much less allowed me to be thrown out of the place, was left with an empty home.

My dad was living in Dana Point in a large townhouse across the street from the ocean with spectacular views. I moved in with him on July 1, 1988.

It wasn't long before Luke came crawling back. He apologized to me and to my father. He promised never to do anything to hurt me ever again and begged me to come home. Like a pregnant, love-sick fool, I went back with him.

On March 9, 1989, just after our one-year anniversary, I gave birth to our gorgeous son Logan.

I was twenty-one years old. I was a good wife with so much love to give, and now I was a mother to this precious little boy. I truly believed everything was going to work out, especially because Luke was thrilled to be a new father. We went to church every Sunday as a family. Our relationship improved and we started having fun together. My body snapped back from giving birth so fast I won a Miss Wild West bikini contest competition six weeks after giving birth. I then went on to win the state championship.

Everything was great, that was until Luke started drinking again. When he drank, the *other* Luke came out and he began to go out and womanize. One night, he came home drunk, thought I wasn't listening to what he was saying, and kicked my nail polish, which flew all over the curtains. That sent him into a rage and he not only gave me a black eye but threw me in a scalding shower. I ended up in the hospital, with my eyes swollen shut. My only recollection was the sound of my mom, quietly sobbing and stroking my hair, saying over and over again, "My baby, my baby."

I had a baby and had to provide a good environment, so I filed for divorce and took Logan.

# Dana Pointless

While I was in Houston falling and failing in love, and Brad was off on his mission, Jason and Carrie remained in the so-called care of my father.

Carrie had a scooter accident while Dad was in jail. She sustained a bloody head injury and was rushed to the hospital where she had to spend the night.

No one was around to visit her.

Thankfully, my sister recovered. As expected, Dad sued the insurance company when he got out of jail and went on to negotiate a settlement on her behalf. In the meantime, he gave Carrie seven dollars in dimes for lunch because that was all he had. He came home from Nadia's (where he mostly stayed) one day because there was no food in the house. He could only afford to restock with five boxes of cereal, milk, and biscuits. Carrie had a birthday present she wanted to mail down to Mom, but he wouldn't give her the money for the postage.

That June, Jason graduated from Laguna Beach High School. He'd applied for college at BYU Hawaii and his girlfriend's family threw a huge graduation luau in his honor. The only problem was he'd actually been rejected. He was embarrassed that he had to go to his other choice, BYU Ricks in Idaho. At the time, it was a two year college, and he felt he had to keep the lie going.

As summer started, Dad, who'd been down on his luck all spring, was suddenly driving around in a 1987 red Mercedes 560SL he'd supposedly repossessed. Never mind that Carrie went into the local pro shop to pick up her tennis racquet and was accused of stealing the strings Dad had brought home and told her to use to have it restrung.

In Fall, 1987, Jason took off via Greyhound bus for BYU Ricks college in Rexburg, Idaho.Once in school, he wrote the following note to Grandfather, who sent him the $1000 per month he provided all of his grandchildren pursuing higher education:

*College is great and I'm having a great time. I'm taking my G. E. classes write now. Psychology— Business law—Practicum—English— history and book of Mormon. College seems so much easier than High School so far... I'm learning the real meaning of studying... I love you a lot and appreciate the things you do for me.*

He added a P.S. requesting a set of scriptures for church and his book of Mormon class.

Not long after he left however, the police showed up at the door looking for Jason. He had a warrant out for his arrest because he'd been caught speeding in the Mercedes and had used his Texas license. In other words, he gave a false address. Dad taught us that you could get a driver's license in multiple states because they didn't connect them like they do today. If we got pulled over, we were to give them a different address. The *beauty* was that if you had too many tickets in California, you just use your license from another state. My brother took up the practice young and had lots of tickets for speeding or for expired registrations. Carrie told them he was away at school and gave them his contact information so they could deal with him directly.

Somehow, the matter got dropped.

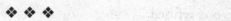

In early October 1987, Dad was sentenced to another twenty days in jail, supposedly due to a parole violation. On October 28, 1987, the case was continued until November 13, and Dad was not released. As it turned out, he had additional counts against him including stealing items from a car.

Carrie was left alone again, so she went to live with one of my mom's friends and her family—a good environment in which she could flourish.

Dad got out of jail soon after and was, as expected, in a rage that my sister was gone. He told me to convince her to come home. He had Jason call her to say she needed to go live with Dad because she wouldn't get a car or money, and that she was going to get disowned. When she called me crying, I told her to live wherever she was happy and sent her $100. My mom agreed and encouraged her to stay.

Despite his pressure and threat campaign, Carrie held her ground, especially after Mom started sending her money for expenses. While she came up for visits, particularly when I came into town, Carrie wanted to be where she was loved and felt secure. Dad eventually accepted her choice, even letting her take the Bronco back and forth, sometimes filling it with gas, and even handing her a twenty or a fifty at the end of a visit.

There were other positive interactions—a father-daughter dance, family holidays, etc., but visiting wasn't without its risks. Dad was forever upset at Carrie for one thing or another and was always trying to persuade her to sign over the upcoming payout from her old scooter accident so he could "invest it" for her.

She refused.

One time, I went to lunch with Carrie in Laguna when Logan was an infant. Carrie and I got in an accident, which was my fault. We got hit in an intersection. The approaching car hit the passenger door where Carrie was sitting, just missing Logan who was in his car seat behind her. Carrie hit the passenger side window and cut her head. She was bleeding profusely but wasn't badly injured. Dad came to the scene and told us to "get into the ambulance and tell them you are really hurt." He followed us to the hospital to make sure we said fake names and fake birthdays. He would always grab us around the waist and you could just feel him digging into your skin if you didn't say the right thing. He'd pull you really close and start squeezing you, or he'd give you a look across the room and you knew you had to lie. It's before they could track all this stuff by computer, so the lies he made us tell almost always worked.

Ironically, the emergency room was filled with cousins because one of them had sustained an ear injury flying home from college from Utah and everyone was saying our real names which made lying impossible.

On another occasion, Dad told Carrie to bring the Bronco back up to the Dana Hills apartment, park it, put the keys in the gas door, and close it. She did exactly that and then jumped on the train back to San Diego.

"Where's the Bronco?" he asked a few days later.

"I dropped it off where you told me, I put the keys there, and that was it. I don't know where the Bronco is!"

He was furious and blamed her. "You can't even take care of a car? Where did you put the Bronco?" He razzed her about it all the time from then on.

Fifteen years later and living in Utah, Carrie went out to lunch with Jason's best friend from high school.

"Do you know what happened to the Bronco way back when?" he asked.

She didn't, so he told her that when Carrie brought the Bronco up, Jason had come home from college for the weekend. He knew the hiding places for keys, so he took it, picked up his friend and they went four-wheeling up in the hills. While they were out joy riding, they flipped it. They jumped out and left it there.

Dad blamed Carrie forever and Jason never admitted what he'd done.

In June 1989, Carrie graduated from high school. She'd lettered in four sports. She decided to attend a Mormon college. Brad, who'd returned from his mission in Fall of 1988, joined Carrie at college, got his degree, and met his wife-to-be.

Despite it all, the Brown bonds would remain weirdly solid.

# On a Mission

The Mormon way is to go to college for a year, go on a mission if at all possible, finish college and/or find someone to marry, then start having kids. For boys, the mission is a two-year assignment. For girls it's a year and a half.

The loving, thankful, sensitive, and kind part of Jason truly wanted to tow the Mormon line. To qualify for a mission, Jason had to have a temple recommend, which meant he had to take a lot of tests, demonstrate his faith in the teachings of Joseph Smith, stay morally and ethically pure, and have the desire to spread the gospel of Mormonism. It helped that Grandfather was a former church bishop, and an LDS High Priest. He could cut through with whatever red tape necessary to confer the title of "elder" upon Jason.

As an elder, Jason had the authority to preside over a family, receive direct communications from God, to teach, and to proselytize. He was able to bestow blessings of health and comfort by laying hands on a recipient's head and praying. He was even authorized to perform the Mormon ritual of baptizing the dead. In other words, he was ready to go on his mission.

Jason's assignment came by mail to him and 25,000 other soon-to-be missionaries in June 1988, weeks before his nineteenth birthday.

He was headed for Paris, France.

"He has set a good example for his church, family, and friends," our local LDS newspaper wrote about his appointment to France. "He is sensitive to the needs and feelings of others and gives unselfishly of his time and efforts to help people."

Jason's mission started at the LDS training center in Provo, Utah with several thousand fellow missionaries. The training involved long hours studying scriptures and LDS books, learning how to teach Mormon doctrine, worshipping in the temple, and foreign language training. During this time, and throughout his mission, Jason wrote frequent letters (filled with grammatical and spelling errors) to Grandfather and Grandmother about his experiences:

*I awakened at 4:00 AM this morning so that I was to make to the temple for my second time this week. I really enjoyed it my second time probably because I was more relaxed of all my 19 years of life I never expected to be like it was. It was very special to me. My biggest goal at the M.T.C. is to follow the rules so that I can be the best missionary I can be. (So far so good.). I've really gained a testimony for prayer... Yes, I do spend a lot of time on my knees. But it's the best way to become closer to our Heavenly Father. I'm really learning a lot about (self-dicipline) probably because I've really havn't had any in my life...I've really never studied so hard in my life, like I have in the past week. There are 10 elders going to Paris. (We call ourselves the Gifted Ones!)*

Jason left for Paris on November 7 with a suitcase Grandfather bought him and filled with the items required on the packing list: walking shoes, ties, white long-sleeved shirts, and two suits. He and his fellow missionaries were taken to the training center at 23 Rue

Du Onze, where they adhered to a daily schedule that started at 6:30 AM and ended every evening with lights out at 10:30 PM.

Missionaries work nine hours a day, six days a week, in same-sex pairs. They live with a companion and are together with that person at all times, except when they go to the bathroom. They never address each other by first name but by "elder" and their last name, as in Elder Brown. Flirting, much less dating, is forbidden. Any missionary caught having sex is sent home. TV, magazines, newspapers, movies, and secular music aren't allowed.

Jason wrote: *I was really worried about who my companion was going to be. But everything worked out and my companion and I get along very well. I really look forward to teaching the gospel in Paris and can't wait.*

The goal of every missionary is to baptize converts, as many as possible. Once they find someone who would listen to the teachings of Joseph Smith, they give their own spiritual testimony, pray with the "investigators" (as potential converts are called) and read scripture, sing hymns, or do kindnesses for them. They never leave a prospective convert without leaving a copy of the Book of Mormon behind.

Once a week, missionaries have time for personal activities on what is known as P-day or Preparation day. On his P-days, Elder Brown wrote regular notes to Grandfather and Grandmother:

*23 Rue du Onze, Novembre*

*…I go to the temple once a week and this week I had the chance to do (sealings) for the dead it was so great! I never thought Jason would start*

*changing but he is, in so many ways. I never thought I could be such a*
*(goody good) but I am (now)…*

*I love you so much.*

Instead of *Love, your grandson*, an omitted comma in his sign offs
sounded more like a command:

*Love your grandson,*
*Elder Brown*

*January 28, 1989*

*Sometimes I wonder where I would be if it wasn't for our big strong*
*family to help me out: I've been through a lot and have learned a lot*
*about life but I have learned so much in the last few months, I'm really*
*looking forward to what's up ahead of me.*

*There are days that are really, really tough when no one wants to lis-*
*ten to us and you just wonder what's this all about. Then there are days*
*that you have a baptism and your on top of the world wishing you never*
*had to come down.*

*May 4, 1989*

*…Well this Sunday we have 3 baptizms: were really excited. I know*
*that doesn't sound like much but if you were a member of a branch with*
*15 members—3 baptizms would mean the world to you…Baptizms are*
*what makes a mission so great: I just love the feeling that I get doing it: I*

*wish I could be baptized again…I don't know how my testimony can get any bigger or stronger? I love to study the Gospel everyday: I never knew the church could be so true!*

After Paris, Jason was transferred three hours southwest to Blois on the Loire River. By that summer, he was living in Saint-Brieve, in Brittany, on the English Channel. Jason was jubilant when a Book of Mormon he left at a home with an interested woman resulted in the conversion of an entire family:

*June 28, 1989*

*…She read the whole Book of Mormon in one week and prayed the second week and received her answer. We baptized her and the family a month later in the ocean. It was a great experience!!! That is one experience I have had that I know that God does prepare people to receive the Gospel.*

On July 1, he turned twenty, and was given a birthday party by the family, but admitted in his next letter that everything wasn't entirely conversions and spiritual bliss:

*7/22/89*
*Well, I think I have met the toughest time of my mission… the work has been going very slow. We have not taught a person the first discussion in almost a month: Yes: you could say that is quite depressing… We've been knocking on doors and doing everything possible to find new people to teach the Gospel to but (no one is interested) It's been really tough on*

*me cause I've had so much success in the early months of my mission...
Well as you can see: Things are tough... but I like the saying "A mission
is like a roller coaster. You have your ups and downs." I'm down "but I'll
get back up and move right along.*

9-7-89

*The work is going absolutely perfect her in my new ville: There is a
big branch of about 65 people: I know that is not a lot but for France,
it's great: The last 3 days have been nothing but teaching people all day
long,*

By November, a year and two months into his mission, he'd been
sent to Orleans.

*November 16, 1989*

*It's really incredible how much the Lord has blessed me on my mis-
sion: I've been really blessed and I also wonder why me? Why have I been
chosen to teach and Baptize these families: I wonder what have I done
to deserve this.*

*Well, I make missionary life sound so easy. I must say: I still have
many trials and difficult times: But, I know that those trials are their to
build me to become a stronger person. As I look back over the last year:
It's been tough: But wouldn't trade it for the world...*

After being transferred from Orleans to Le Havre, he wrote:

*1-18-90*

*I love to watch people change their lives to do good and come unto Christ... I love being a missionary: I love to feel so close to the heavenly father... It's great to feel his spirit so often: I've learned that the only way to find true happiness in this life is by following the commandment and doing what our heavenly father wants us to do.*

Then, he was sent to Troyes, a couple hours southeast of Paris:

*March 29, 1990*

*My new ville is right on the border of the Brussel Belgium Mission... (I'm baptizing people all the time) and most of all, I'm being good: Sometimes that's a big job for Elder Brown but now it's just a (habit).*

There are many letters, and they are all startlingly similar, like Jason was trying hard to gain approval by proving he'd embarked on a new chapter in his life. I think Jason wrote all those letters to my grandparents because my dad was in and out of jail and didn't have money to send him like Grandfather, who had funded the mission. Jason felt indebted to him enough to write what seem to be heartfelt notes.

Jason knew he had an evil side to him. Usually sociopaths don't even have that other side. When they do, it's fake. With Jason it was real. In retrospect, it's not surprising that Jason tried so hard to be good, or that he and Grandfather had a closer relationship than I realized. Given my grandfather passed along whatever bad blood was in his genetic code to my dad, who then passed it along to Jason, it was like Stockholm Syndrome (otherwise known as the Betrayal Bond) amongst narcissists and sociopaths.

# MARRIED MAN

Jason, who was 5'8" with his shoes on, had a thing for tall, beautiful women. While on his mission, he met a stunning, leggy, 5'11" blonde fellow missionary named Laura. Incredibly, she was the same Laura who happened to be one of my close friends from college.

Laura left college when I did. She went home to the East Coast, decided to go on a mission, and was assigned to Paris. There, ironically, she met Elder Brown—and had no idea he was my brother. Jason was immediately drawn to Laura's looks, her beautiful singing voice, and her intelligence. She found him fun, funny, generous, and loved that he claimed to want the whole Mormon lifestyle—the wedding, the babies, all of it. Because she'd had a rough childhood of her own, they seemed to be perfectly suited for each other.

The mission president saw what was going on and separated them immediately, sending them to opposite sides of France. The distance only caused their feelings to grow. In late summer, 1990, when Jason's mission ended, Laura was already back in the States and they were still madly in love. Supposedly ready to begin the adult life of a devout Mormon, he and Laura got engaged quickly soon after.

They married on May 25, 1991 at the Los Angeles Temple. In temple weddings, the bride and groom kneel on opposite sides of the altar, holding hands while they are sealed by a church elder in the

Celestial Room. Large mirrors hang from opposite walls so couples can turn and gaze into their endless "eternal" joined reflections. Only temple-worthy Mormons can watch, while everyone else, even relatives, must wait outside. Mom came in from Texas and my dad was there, but Grandfather served as witness and signed the marriage certificate. After the ceremony, we all drove back to Orange County for a reception at the Dana Point Recreational Facility which is on the water in Dana Point Harbor where my dad lived.

Three-year-old Logan looked absolutely adorable in his tux.

Only Carrie, who was in Thailand teaching English, missed Jason's wedding. Dad insisted she come home for the event, but having paid $1,000 to get there, she simply couldn't afford to come back. She also didn't much feel like following his orders any longer. Just before she'd left the country, she heard he'd been talking about her behind her back and was furious at him. When he began yelling at her on the phone about coming to the wedding and tried to bribe her to come back home by telling her he'd finally gotten the $10,000 from the insurance settlement for her scooter accident, she said she didn't care. In fact, she'd had enough and said, "I never want to see or speak to you again."

She not only didn't ever see or speak to him again, but when she came home, she tracked down the accident report, figured out the insurance company of the person who hit her, and contacted them. She learned that Dad had tried to claim the check but since Carrie was an adult, he couldn't get his hands on it.

They sent the money directly to her.

Dad had ostracized Carrie for her disloyalty to him and Jason towed the line, so my brother and sister were somewhat estranged at the time of the wedding. Unlike me, she never received a letter from him for the two years he was gone to France. Besides, Jason, who was twenty-three and fresh off his mission, had his hands too full with the expectations of his white-picket fence future to worry too much about whether Carrie was in attendance or not.

Laura and Jason settled in Monterey, California where he'd been admitted to an MBA program at the Monterey Institute of International Studies, a multicultural graduate and professional school with a tuition of $30,000. He needed no formal degree to get in but had to take the GMAT and prove proficiency in a foreign language. He was fluent in French so he qualified for the program.

Laura worked at Pebble Beach teaching aerobics, which enabled Jason to play golf for free. Jason was able to schmooze his professors by taking them to play there. He looked like a cultured lad, and reveled in his big-shot image, but it was all a front. Dad kept getting Jason to take loans out through his school saying, "I'll pay you back after you graduate."

It may have been the beginning of Jason's downfall because Dad didn't pay him back and Jason got more and more in debt. He also struggled with school, having only gone to college for a year. Laura, who was super smart, wrote all of his papers. She was willing because he was her husband and she wanted him to succeed.

Jason and I didn't get along as children, but when he came back from his mission and married Laura, I used to bring Logan to visit them in Monterey. During that time we grew very close.

Even though Jason and Laura seemed like the perfect couple with a bright future ahead, Jason was growing anxious. Soon after they were married, my mom asked Jason, "When are you guys having kids?"

"I'm never going to have kids because they're going to end up just like me," he said. "And I wouldn't want that to happen to any kid."

Laura, on the other hand, wanted to start a family right away.

Tensions grew high between them.

A lot of Mormon kids get married at a young age and start having children of their own. Sometimes, they don't know what hit them when it happens and then they're stuck. Jason was one of those kids. He married too young and felt like he had more life to live. He wanted to go out and explore other options. He didn't want to be tied down.

They were together just long enough for him to graduate from Monterey Institute on May 7, 1995. Soon after, Jason walked out saying he just didn't want to be married. He was twenty-six.

After she divorced my brother, Laura remarried, had three children, and they bought a house on Hillview Drive in Laguna Beach—the very street where we'd grown up. I was taken aback, but I can only assume she probably felt duped by my brother—walked out on and shamed. She had a point to prove to Laguna Beach and the Brown name. What better way than to move back to the very place where things unraveled for the Brown family?

# Risky Business

After Jason left Laura, he moved back down to Newport Beach and started to see how fun life could be. He rented a killer house in Beacon Bay and transformed from being a married, "true believing" Mormon into a flashy, showy party boy who was all about appearances.

He quickly accumulated tons of friends who loved to hang out with him, drink, and enjoy the $95,000 Porsche convertible and other assorted toys that soon filled his immaculate garage. People were drawn to his outgoing personality and his constant desire to have fun at all times. He was always taking someone out to ride his ATV, motorcycle, or for a weekend of boating at Lake Havasu.

Whenever we would be out on the lake or towing his "toys" and one of his friends would make a mean comment about someone else's "heap of crap" boat or ATV, Jason always said, "Don't make fun of other people's fun."

I liked that about Jason.

What I didn't like as much was how he was making the money to fund his lifestyle. Jason, like my dad, loved the casinos. Jason would take me with him to Vegas and gamble all night. I'd go to sleep, wake up, and go downstairs and he'd still be at the blackjack table. He could easily turn $2000 into $20,000 in an evening. The casinos comped him and treated him like the high roller he'd become. I remember hanging out with him in the room and just throwing money up in the air.

His income came from two sources: the first was gambling and it disappeared as quickly as he won it. If he won big in Vegas, he'd take everyone out to dinner and pay for everybody's rooms. He was very generous. My highlight was always the shopping sprees. His second source of income was from fake lines of credit. Jason had a birth certificate he'd doctored up with white-out and an old typewriter font, changing dates where needed. He'd learned it all from my dad, starting with Little League when he changed a birth certificate so Jason could play on a younger team and be better. Jason found the birth certificate that had been changed and used it to create a completely different person. His name was still Jason Derek Brown, but he was born a year later. He got a completely different Social Security number for that person and used it for speeding tickets and fake credit. In order to rent a new place, he used his good credit when necessary and would falsify bank statements or bank applications. I don't think he ever paid taxes either. I know my dad never did. When he had to do loan applications, Jason would go to the library, get tax forms, falsify all of his information, and then make a photocopy to make it look like it was filed with the IRS.

My dad always had a wad of cash with a money clip. When he was short on cash, the outside would be quite a few hundreds, then smaller denominations followed and the inside would be ones, but he would always toss it on the table for show. Jason did the same thing.

While living this high on money that wasn't theirs should have been incredibly stressful, narcissistic sociopaths don't think like normal people. They don't have emotion. They don't have regret. They don't experience pain. They'll console you or be empathetic towards you about something or act like they care, but they don't. They're really good at putting on a show of whatever they need to portray. My father was a compulsive, obsessive, sex-addicted, narcissist, sociopath, gambling addict. My brother had become a much more likeable, downright charming version of exactly the same thing.

It worked as long as he was willing to stay on the move.

Given staying in one spot felt all wrong for either of us, he had no problem moving on. When he sensed it was time, he left his good-time pals in Newport Beach and moved to the Sugar House neighborhood in Salt Lake City and started up the fun all over again.

Jason had a knack for getting what and who he wanted. He definitely had a Napoleon complex, and only dated tall, really beautiful women. Despite wearing lifts in his shoes, Jason's charm trumped his height. He had tons of girlfriends and was always causing problems because he'd get caught cheating on the regular. One girl put signs all over his lawn that said, *A dog lives here, cheater,* and all sorts of other screwed up stuff. While women were constantly coming and going, he did have a serious relationship in Salt Lake City with a really beautiful model. She was lovely and came from a nice family. I have a photo book she made him of all their times together. She came out to California to play golf with all of us. He didn't cheat on her for the year they were together.

After that relationship ended, Jason moved from Salt Lake City back to Newport Beach. Then, he moved to Phoenix.

# SINGLE MOM

I was a single, unemployed mom. Being a flight attendant wouldn't work with a small child and I needed a flexible job where I could support myself and care for my son. One day, I picked up a copy of a business magazine called DBA. It was slick, beautiful, and had high-end advertisers. Even though I had no experience, I went to the headquarters of the magazine on the top floor of an office building in downtown Houston and asked for the director of sales.

"Do you have an appointment?" the receptionist asked.

"No," I admitted, "but I'm really interested in a sales position."

I must have seemed as enthusiastic as I felt because she went ahead and called the sales manager. A few minutes later, a blond woman in her twenties (and who happened to fit my general description) appeared in the reception area.

"I'm Natalie, the director of sales. How can I help you?"

"I'm Jami Martin and I'd like to interview for a job."

"Do you have a resume?"

"I don't," I said.

"Sales experience?"

"I know I'm perfect for this."

"Go home and write up a resume," she said. "Bring it back to my office on Monday."

179

Since I had no actual sales experience, I came back that Monday with a resume that contained every job I'd ever worked, from flight attendant to working at the candy store in Laguna. We both knew I wasn't exactly qualified, but thankfully, she saw something in me and gave me a job.

"You won't be sorry," I told her.

In less than a year, I was the top sales producer. I sold advertising spots for both television and print and had a knack for picking up big clients that included Mercedes Benz and BMW dealerships. Not only did I have a way with the general managers, but one of them put me in the print ad for his dealership. Another co-signed for me so I could buy a BMW. I'm sure it helped that I was blonde, bold, and flirtatious because nine times out of ten, they were buying whatever I was selling. All my life I'd been controlled financially by the men in my life. Legitimately earning money felt amazing. I didn't have to depend on anybody. I could take care of myself. I loved the independence of earning my own income and being my own person.

While my career was going incredibly well and I reveled in being a mother to Logan, my interactions with my ex-husband became increasingly difficult. Luke was a really good-looking guy and everybody was in love with him which still hurt. He would pick Logan up for visitation and I would hear the never-ending stories about what and who he was doing. There was the property manager, the married wife of one of his friends, and then a porn star he'd met when she appeared as a featured performer at one of the strip clubs I now knew he frequented.

Following his break-up with the porn star, we tried again to work things out for Logan's sake, but I knew in my heart I couldn't live with him. It ended quickly. He started dating a woman who was a bodybuilding fitness fanatic and they moved in together. Somehow, seeing him settle down was easier to deal with then having him run around with random women.

Not long after, Luke began to drop weight and had signs of a weakened immune system. He found out he was HIV positive and had been infected by the porn star. I was utterly terrified but thankfully, we'd used protection and I remained healthy. His relationship with the new woman fell apart as a result. Luke met another woman, who, despite his diagnosis, married and took care of him. She saw me as a threat and wanted nothing to do with having me around even though Luke and I were committed to raising a child together.

The stress of his situation was unbearable and I was very worried about the effects on Logan of seeing his father getting sicker and weaker, so I moved back to California and, temporarily, back in with my father.

Dad, being Dad, immediately pulled me into his nonsense. One day, he told me to meet him in a Laguna parking lot and wait for him. Why I agreed I can't say, especially when he told me to back out of my parking space. As I did, he hit my car on purpose and then filed a claim against my insurance company saying he was injured. He was out of money, so staging accidents and filing insurance claims was his main source of income.

Thankfully, my boss Natalie quit DBA magazine and moved to Malibu, California soon after I left Houston. She called me immediately. "I'm going to work for a company called Strategic Telecom. Do you want to be one of my sales reps?"

I accepted and was given the San Diego and Orange County markets.

During this time, Jason had moved back to Orange County. I was working hard, but Jason always seemed to have free time. I knew something was up but chose to accept the party line that he and Brad and Jason had started a golf advertising business.

I loved being a mom and did everything for Logan. He never took the bus because I drove him to school every day. I was the team mom for every sport. I drove him to every practice and made sure I had the best birthday parties for him. I was beyond protective of my beautiful boy.

Luke would fly out to California to spend time with our son. Every time he visited, he looked worse than the time before. When Logan was five, Luke came out for a visit which startled me. Once 220 pounds with a bodybuilder's physique, he was now painfully thin and had carcinomas all over his skin. So little was known in those days about AIDS. We both recognized his life had a time limit, we just did not know he was so close to the end.

I still have the photos of them playing on the beach in Diver's Cove in Laguna Beach on that cold winter day. Logan had on a red cotton long sleeve shirt and jeans, while Luke had on blue jeans and a green and blue checkered flannel shirt with a hood. I watched them in the distance as they ran back and forth on the shoreline, laughing. Luke would periodically pick him up and swing him around in the air or sit on the sand with his arms wrapped around our son. Time stopped during those moments, knowing Logan was unaware of Luke's deteriorating condition. He only saw his Dad, not the illness.

It would be the last time Logan or I would see him alive.

Soon after, I got a call from his mother. Luke had gone down to Mexico, caught a parasite, and his immune system couldn't fight it off.

"You need to come to Texas right now. Luke's not going to make it."

I was at the airport getting on the plane when I got the call that he'd died.

I felt powerless. I was also sad, scared, numb, anxious, mad, and hurt. I was not prepared emotionally, but I knew I had to get strong and pull it together so I could find the words to tell Logan his dad was dead.

Later that day, as the sun was setting, I put Logan in the car and we headed down to Diver's Cove beach on Cliff Drive in Laguna Beach. We went to the exact spot where just months prior, we had spent that winter day. We found some big rocks to sit on and stared out into the vast blue ocean and watched the sun head down into the horizon.

"Logan," I said, holding him close and tight. "Mommy has something to tell you that is really hard and I want you to know that everything is going to be okay."

Logan looked just like Luke as he gazed up at me with total trust.

"Logan, your Dad went to live with the angels up there." I pointed to the sky. "He went to heaven."

I don't know how a five year old processes death, or how he understood that his Dad was gone, but he knew exactly what I was saying.

I held my beautiful blonde baby boy as he sobbed.

Luke's funeral was scheduled for the day of my sister Carrie's wedding. After returning from Thailand, she reconnected with her church youth group from college and met a returned missionary. They fell in love and set a date. I'd been looking forward to being there for months. Instead, I was a twenty-five-year-old divorcee/widow with a five-year-old son, and one of three former wives in attendance at the funeral for my ex-husband who was dead from AIDS.

We were seated in the first row of a packed church staring at Luke's closed casket. I remember feeling grateful to be able to remember him as the big, handsome, strong man and father he'd been.

Every attendee was given a red rose to hold until after "Bed of Roses" by Bon Jovi was played. It was one of Luke's favorite songs. As soon as the song was over, we were to go up and place our flower on his casket and say our final goodbyes. Mid-song, I whispered to Logan, "Do you want to be the first to say goodbye to your Dad?"

Logan, who was incredibly brave throughout the ceremony, stood holding his rose. Dressed in his black suit and tie with shiny black loafers, and looking every bit the angel he was, my precious five-year-old walked alone up the stairs to the casket in full view of everyone and place the rose on his Dad's casket.

Quiet sobs echoed throughout the church.

Following the service, Luke's sister literally yanked Logan from me, threw him in a limo, and took him to the gravesite. I followed in my car, located my son, and we got out of there.

I never told my son how his father died until recently. Instead, I said he had cancer and had died from a parasite because of his weakened immune system. Logan had already been through too much and our losses were just getting started.

# JAMES

I did my best to keep busy in the aftermath of Luke's death. Thank God, I had Natalie who had just made me sales manager of the San Diego territory, for Strategic Telecom. I was bopping around to all the high end restaurants and nightclubs selling advertising and loving it.

I commuted back and forth to stay at my dad's so Logan could attend a private school called Anneliese's in Laguna Beach. They had a very creative curriculum and the days were filled with learning languages, cooking, and art classes. Logan could count and speak basic words in Japanese, French, and German. The school was filled with teachers from all over the globe. I was grateful to receive Luke's $1000 per month social security benefits for Logan. They enabled me to afford the monthly tuition.

My mom used to call Logan, "The Golden Child." At first, she was joking, but other members in the family started to as well. The name stuck. I was overprotective of Logan, almost to the point of obsession. I had to protect him at all costs. That was my job now that his dad was gone. He had horrible nightmares after Luke's death. So did I, but I didn't have time to worry about how I felt anymore. I just had to keep moving forward and take care of Logan.

That summer, Mom suggested that Logan spend the summer with her, so I could focus on work and stay the week in San Diego instead of making the hour drive back and forth every night. That sounded like a good idea and I knew Logan would be in good hands.

My mom loved having her beautiful grandson to dote on, although she was afraid I would freak out if he got a scratch or scuffed knee on her watch. She wasn't wrong, but she ran her own daycare so I knew he was safe and Logan would have plenty of kids to play with. The daycare knew he was "The Golden Child" and the shining star there. My mom took him everywhere she went and adored him.

I was able to dive hard into work to keep my mind occupied and save money to get my own place in Laguna.

One day, my mom walked into Logan's bedroom and saw he looked sad.

"I hope my mom hasn't died," he said.

My mom rushed over, knelt down next to him, and hugged him. "No, sweetheart, your mom is fine! She is just working."

Mom took him to the home phone and they called me right away so I could reassure him. He had lost his dad, and now he thought everyone died and went away.

Unfortunately, his experience with loss was far from over.

Not long after Luke's death, I was in a valet parking line, getting into my car. Nearby, a man in a red Porsche was opening the door for his date. As we were walking to the drivers' sides of our respective cars, he handed me his card and said, "Give me a call."

"What about the girl in the car?" I asked, looking over at the really beautiful woman now sitting in the passenger seat, entirely unaware of what he was saying to me.

"She's just a friend," he said.

"She certainly doesn't look like just a friend."

"Call me," he said.

Intrigued, I called him and he admitted she was actually his girl-friend of five years but that the relationship was all but over. We went out a few times and he did, in fact, break up with her. Like Luke, James was also ten years older than me, but he had never been married. He and Logan adored each other from the first time I finally introduced them to each other six months after we'd met. He also loved and wanted to marry me. I loved him, but not in the way I had Luke, mainly because I was so shut down after watching him die.

"You need to marry James," my dad kept saying. "He's a great guy and Logan needs a father."

"I don't want to marry him," I insisted, afraid of facing any more loss.

"James loves you. He loves your son."

"I know," I said. "But—"

"Love is something that grows," he said, delivering a bit of un-characteristically wise advice. "Marry him."

I wasn't head over heels with James the way I had been with Luke, but I knew my dad was right. In March 1994, James and I eloped to Hawaii.

Even though I went back and forth with the church, I still sought approval from my family, so I had Luke and James both baptized. I didn't marry Mormons, but I could certainly make my partners into Mormons, which made everyone, especially my mother, happy.

James was a good guy, a great husband, and an even better father figure for Logan. He was honest, a successful entrepreneur, not addicted to porn, and didn't cheat on me. While I didn't feel the butterflies I had for Luke, I did have something I'd never had before—security. Without James, we both may have never made it. He was the blessing that God put into our life.

# John Brown is Missing

If you google David John Brown, you will find a link to the California missing persons and the following information: *David John Brown Sr. was last seen in Dana Point, California on September 1, 1994. He left his residence after telling his family to sell everything because he wasn't coming back. He has never been heard from again.*

*Brown may be driving a white 1992 Nissan Infiniti Q45 with no license plates. Few details are available in his case.*

I have no idea who owned the Infinity he was driving at the time, much less what happened to my dad.

Six months earlier, Dad was babysitting Logan at his place. My son loved hanging out with his grandpa and my dad loved being with Logan. Having lost his father not a year earlier, this was a critical bond. When I came to pick Logan up at the end of the evening, Dad sat down on the staircase, and leaned back into the wall to support his back. He seemed exhausted and started rambling.

"You know, it's really hard to make a living Jami," he said darkly. "It's really hard to make it out there."

"What are you talking about?" At the time he was trying to make a go of a golf apparel company called Duffy with a logo featuring a cartoonish character holding a golf ball. I figured it wasn't going too well. Dad never talked about anything being wrong or life being too challenging, and he seemed uncharacteristically depressed.

"Life's really tough," he said. He kept repeating himself, as if to convince himself. "It's really hard to make money."

I was thinking *no, it's not*. I was working and doing really well, but decided it was best to listen and not argue that it's only hard to make money when you're a con artist. I figured his moment of weakness had less to do with an existential crisis on his part and more that his lies were somehow catching up with him. We'd all noticed he'd gotten sloppier and I thought maybe he was starting to crack. It wasn't the first time he'd started talking crazy and he'd been rambling about stuff, particularly involving my mom, belaboring every point, and talking in circles. He'd always lied, but suddenly he wouldn't hesitate to look you in the eye and repeat a detailed story he'd told you the day before in a completely different way.

"You didn't say that yesterday," I'd say.

"Yeah, I did," he'd argue.

"No," I'd say and repeat exactly what he'd said the day before.

He'd act like I didn't know what I was talking about.

I thought maybe he was struggling to keep track of his various lies or starting to lose it altogether. Then again, narcissists and sociopaths do have weak moments where they break down and reveal glimpses of humanity. The mask falls off and they are shown for what they are briefly before they collect themselves and go back to business as usual.

Things did get back to normal, and I honestly didn't think all that much about it all. He seemed his usual self—gambling, and living large with Karen, the most recent "love of his life." Karen was a married mom with two young kids who weren't yet teenagers. My Dad would follow Karen and her husband on dates to the movies, sit two rows behind them, and spy on them until Karen left her husband for my Dad. He gave her a huge diamond ring soon after. They had an engagement party at the Ritz-Carlton. He even flew in her best friend from Japan to surprise her.

On Sunday afternoon, August 28, 1994, I'd gotten home from three hours of church and was trying to take a rest, a rarity for me.

I was woken up by the distinctive sound of my dad's red convertible Cobra with white racing stripes. It was a kit car, but everyone thought it was the real thing and he was very into driving it around. Irritable from having my nap interrupted, I went out onto the balcony. "What are you doing here?"

"I just came by to see if everything was okay."

"Everything's fine. Why would you come over here to ask me that question?" I answered feeling cranky.

"Want to go for a Sunday drive?" My dad asked.

"No! I'm sleeping and you're bothering me for no reason."

"I just want to make sure everything is ok."

"Ok with what?"

"Ok with James and Logan."

"Everything is fine. I am fine. We are fine."

"If you want me to take a drive with you, call first. Don't just show up," I said, completely irritated that my dad had chosen the one time I'd dozed off to be fatherly. I knew my dad genuinely cared about all of us, but it was always about him, on his time.

"Everything is fine!" I said, irritated.

He drove off, but I knew I'd see him in four days for Friday surprise party I was having to celebrate James's upcoming birthday.

Little did I know, I would never see him again.

I had every detail of the surprise party planned down, from the cake to the adult party favors. I love entertaining and I had a natural talent for it.

Karen showed up early to help.

"Where is Dad?" I asked.

"He said he would be here later," she said, which meant he was either playing golf or up to no good, and would, of course be late, as usual.

My dad never showed up that night.

"I know where he is," Karen finally said. "He's cheating on me again!"

Despite getting engaged to my dad, Karen was no dummy. Whether it was running back and forth to Mexico, using driver's licenses from multiple states, shoplifting, or dying his hair black *just for fun*, John Brown was always up to something. It didn't really bother her that he had her charge everything on her credit card and then paid her back in cash—including his gall bladder surgery—she was most suspicious about him secretly seeing other women.

As the evening came to an end, we all sighed and shook our heads. While it definitely wasn't outside the realm of possibility, it wasn't unusual for Dad to disappear for days or even months at a time, although he usually told us when he'd be away.

My brothers shrugged it off. I was so tired of his bullshit and games, I did the same. Only Karen was concerned. After all, she'd left her stable husband for my *charming* dad who gave her gifts, took her on cruises and vacations, and sent her romantic letters. He was attentive enough that she overlooked the inconsistencies in his behavior until this particular disappearance. Apparently, he'd been talking about selling his cars and moving. While they were in Vegas on a getaway weekend, he'd tried switching the registration of his 1992 Infiniti Q45 to Nevada.

Once again, completely normal behavior in our minds.

Karen went over to his house after the party because he hadn't shown up or contacted her. She had a key, but it wouldn't work in the door—once again a surprise to none of us since Dad regularly put keys in doors and would then take a hammer and chop the key off so no one else could put a key in the door and get in. He taught all of us how to do it. I can still hear his words in my head: "If you don't want someone to unlock a door, put your key in, then take a hammer, hit it off, and then no one can get in."

Serious life skills.

There was no sign of my dad.

I came home Sunday after getting a call from Karen saying that Jason and Brad were at the house. I headed over to my dad's house on Chula Vista in Dana Point and was shocked to see a Ryder truck parked in Dad's driveway and my brothers throwing his clothes into the trash cans.

"What in the hell are you doing?" I asked as Jason heaved a new jogging suit I'd bought Dad for Father's Day into the garbage. "I just got that for him."

"He's not coming back," Jason said with no emotion whatsoever.

"What do you mean?" I asked, tears running down my face.

"Dad told us if he wasn't back in twenty-four hours to clean out the house and get rid of everything immediately."

"When did he tell you this?"

"Over twenty-four hours ago."

"Oh, really? Why didn't he say anything to me?"

Brad shrugged. "It was just a general warning."

"He's coming back. He wouldn't just leave forever. He's got a grandson he loves. Logan's just a little kid."

"Twenty-four hours," Jason said, parroting Brad. "We're supposed to get rid of everything."

"How do you know he's really gone? He could come back next week. Just because he said he was going somewhere, it doesn't mean he did, okay?"

They both kept working.

"You guys can't do this," I said, a sick panic welling up in me. "It isn't right. You're throwing his clothes in the trashcan. I don't believe—"

"Jami, he's gone and he's never coming back," Jason said, his gaze cold and dead. "You just need to deal with it."

I watched helplessly as they proceeded to heave anything they thought they could sell into the Ryder truck, even laughing together in the macabre way they often did when things were bad. I never saw any of my Dad's belongings again, just like I would never see a dime from the cars, televisions, furniture and whatever else they hauled away and sold.

All I could do was wish I hadn't been so short with my father when he'd come to my house and asked me if I wanted to take a drive. Maybe, just maybe, he'd have given me some information, a clue, as to what was going on.

The thought devastated me.

# Unfinished Business

Grandfather filed a missing person's report with the Orange County sheriff's department six weeks after Dad disappeared, and only then because the rest of the family pushed him to do so. My dad had distanced himself from his parents and siblings, and Grandfather feared his money problems and penchant for Tijuana gambling had gotten him mixed up with the wrong crowd. Grandfather said, "It was not like John to just leave without explaining his reason," but my dad was the master at disappearing and avoiding people. I honestly think Grandfather hated the burden that my dad was on the family name and was glad he was gone. He probably never even shed a tear.

I was able to locate the following information from the report, not all of which was accurate:

**Reported by: Bernard Brown**
**Date: October 14, 1994**
**Name: David John Brown-**
**Alias or Nickname: John**
**Sex: Male**
**Race: Caucasian**
**Birthdate: 3-4-43**

**Age: 51**

**Weight: 250 lbs**

**Height:6'2**

**Eyes: Brown Eyes** (he had Blue)

**Glasses: No** (He always wore glasses.)

**Hair: Gray balding with Beard** (It was light brown with a gray beard.)

**Religion: None**

**Fingerprint Clarification: None**

**Last seen: Dana Point California driving a 1992 Q 45 Infinity, - color White- with no license plates**

**Clothing Description: Blue Suit** (How did Bernie know what he was wearing? My dad didn't wear suits.)

**Mental/Physical Condition: Good**

**Scars Marks or Tattoos: None**

**Photo Available: None** (Who doesn't have a photo of their child for a missing person's report? I believe this proves Grandfather did not want John Brown found.)

**Probable Destination: Las Vegas**

**Report: A sheriff was dispatched to Via de Agua in San Juan Capistrano in reference to a missing person's report. I met with Bernard Brown who told me the following. His son, David John Brown had been missing since the first part of September 1994. David John told his girlfriend and his daughter Jami to sell everything and he said he won't be back. David John Brown left his residence in a 1992 White Q 45 Infinity (no license plates). David John has not been seen or heard from since the above date (September 1994).**

**Bernard said David John Brown is in good mental condition and does not believe he harmed himself. Bernard said David John's girlfriend hired a private investigator to assist in locating him. It was learned through the private investigator that David John Brown was in Las Vegas on September 19, 1994 at an unknown casino paying off a gambling debt/voucher. Bernard, nor any of his family members can explain the cause of his absence. Bernard said it is not like David John to leave without explaining his reason.**

**I entered in David John Brown into the computer as missing. Chris Catalano Investigating Officer Case # 94-58723**

In the missing person's report, Grandfather told the investigator that Karen had hired a private investigator, and that the P.I. said, "He was last seen in Las Vegas, at an unknown casino paying off gambling debt/voucher."

My dad didn't pay debts to anyone. There was no video surveillance camera footage and no evidence, just another person claiming they saw him. I believe the P.I. made it up to justify his bill.

I later found a letter Dad had written to my grandfather which showed me both sides of their struggle. My Dad never got the approval he needed from his father even as an adult in his 40s and that his love was conditional. Grandfather hated Dad for stealing from him and lying to him. He only helped my Dad when he was in trouble to save the Brown name. Other than that, he just wanted John and his criminal ways out of the picture completely. In Grandfather's eyes, Dad was a disgrace to the family.

*Why do you hate me so much?*
*You could care less about me and my kids.*

*I'm divorced, out of the church and the whole family stomps me to the ground.*

*You all act like good Christian people and yet all of your greediness is sickening*

*You took everything of mine.*
*1. Motor home*
*2. My house*
*3. 100,000*

*Brad stole my things when I was in jail. You stole my furniture when I was in jail and gave it to Brooke. There is no difference.*

*I ask you to be honest and not lie and you still do.*
*Ever since the divorce you have all stomped the shit out of me.*
*I just live day to day to survive. Brooke can do no wrong. You give her everything. She's the biggest gossiper there is. She had nothing. She has everything now.*

*Your love is only conditional. You control and give money to who you want.*

*I get skis, boots, and poles stolen by one of Sherri's kids and you hush it up. I still don't have them back.*

*You've always tried to destroy me.*

*I've stayed away from the family. I don't go near mother. Mother disowned me and she and you only put up a front because of the church.*

*You could care less about my kids. You always provide for Sherri's and Brooke's kids with jobs and everything.*

*Your honesty and fairness is unspeakable.*

*You don't want to deal with any of this. If you want to sell the Bronco too, I don't give a shit.*

*The reason I'm not going back to church ever again is for no other reason than you—*

*You've never been fair and honest with me. I told you not to say anything about me going to jail and all I hear is John's going to jail. No one else knew but you.*

*Jami tells me, Sherri's son tells me all because you tell Brooke and her big mouth is never shut. I will never tell anyone of the family again. I don't give a damn. Goodbye*

(Written Sideways on paper)
*Do I owe you anything? tell me how?*
*I'll tell the Bishop I'm going to jail and to take care of Jason.*

*God how I wish you could have been a fair and honest Father.*

After the report was filed, the Orange County Sheriff's office tried to talk to all of us. Carrie had moved away and hadn't seen Dad in a few years so she had no relevant information. Missing Persons kept trying to interview the boys and they wanted nothing to do with it and didn't particularly cooperate. All three of my siblings had suffered at the hands of our father for far too long which explains, at least in part, why they seemed indifferent to his sudden disappearance. As kids, he'd pulled us into everything and now that we were grown up, he interfered in everything—always causing problems with our marriages and relationships. Still, unlike my siblings, I was a complete basket case. When asked, I told the Orange County sheriff's office what I could, which was to look first in Vegas, but good luck finding him.

All I really knew was that my dad was gone.

Jason came over to my house one afternoon when Logan and James were off at basketball practice. I'd been a basket case since Dad disappeared.

"Why are you acting like this? He's not coming back; do you hear me?" he yelled as I sobbed uncontrollably. "You need to get a hold of yourself!"

When I still didn't calm down, he literally began to shake me. "You need to get it together!"

Because physicality was a means of control in our family, I didn't think all that much of it. Unfortunately, I lost my footing this time, and tumbled down to the first landing on the flight of stairs. I wasn't hurt, just rattled by the whole situation and I became even more emotional.

Two days later, I suffered a miscarriage.

I'd had no idea I was pregnant.

The miscarriage left me that much more traumatized. In my mind, Jason shaking me wasn't weird, and the fact that I'd slipped wasn't his fault. He hadn't meant for me to fall and he certainly didn't know I was pregnant because I didn't even know. In the course of a year, I'd lost an ex-husband to a horrible death, my father had disappeared, and now I'd miscarried. The last thing on my mind was blaming Jason.

As for my dad's disappearance, I wasn't quite so rational. I read somewhere that he'd withdrawn large sums of money from the bank. I knew that wasn't true because he didn't have any money and I don't even think he had a bank account. All he had was the safe in his home office, which held secrets, but little cash.

I had a few theories about what happened to my dad, none of them comforting. The first was that he truly had messed with the wrong people and had warned Brad in advance what was going down. I hated to consider what that meant in terms of what had actually happened to him, but it was definitely believable. My second theory was that Dad planned or staged his own disappearance for similar reasons, possibly even entering a witness protection program. Suicide was another possibility, but narcissists and sociopaths don't usually kill themselves unless they are put in a situation they are unable to come out of.

We'd all noticed he wasn't as quick or able to keep his stories straight. Maybe he knew he was getting soft and couldn't hold his cons together anymore, so he decided he would just disappear and make everyone wonder what ever happened to John Brown. In some ways, it would have been just like my dad to plan the whole thing, letting Jason know so he could tell us, while the rest of the world wondered what happened to him. The one thing that bothered me about that theory was that even though he pulled all kinds of underhanded, manipulative crap, he loved us kids. He always said, "If anybody ever hurts any of you, I'll kill them with my bare hands." Excluding him, of course. He would do anything for us to protect us or give us anything that we wanted. He needed us as much as we needed him.

While the Feds weren't going to tell me if he was in a witness protection program and had been given a new identity, I believe he would have told me something before disappearing. I spent many nights awake, wondering if he would have divulged something to me had I just gone with him on that Sunday drive a few days before he vanished.

In the end, I truly wish that when Jason pushed me down the stairs, he hadn't looked at me with dead, cold eyes like somebody with no conscience. I'd have been greatly reassured if only he'd said something along the lines of, "You know, Dad had to take off somewhere and hide," or, "He's in the witness protection program," or even, "It's okay Jami. I know it's hard for you."

Because he never did, I had to wonder if Dad ever actually said, "If I'm not back in twenty-four hours, get rid of all my stuff." Maybe a fight happened. There were hot tempers in our family and when somebody lost it, they lost it. Although Dad was a big man and definitely not someone to mess with, maybe Jason hit him over the head, dragged his body off, disposed of him, and then made up that story.

Jason's emotionless insistence that Dad was gone forever, and his total lack of interest in searching for him was suspicious. I also think Jason could easily have told Brad something he believed about Dad's whereabouts. Something that explained the stone-cold looks and the jokes as they were throwing my dad's clothes in the trash and loading up anything of value to sell. Neither of them would think to give me or Carrie a dime because, in their minds, we had plenty of money.

Both Jason and Brad resented Dad for everything he'd put them through emotionally, physically, and otherwise. Jason hated our dad for beating him as a kid, but he was furious over adult insults like encouraging him to take out student loans to attend the Monterey Institute of International Business and then promising but failing to pay them back. My dad was always causing conflict and butting his head into places that were clearly none of his business. He got into all of our marriages and caused problems, telling secrets or making up shit to watch us fight. If Jason did do something to our father, maybe that's why he started drinking heavily and doing drugs.

He'd done so many bad things to all of us, but I still loved my dad and I felt abandoned.

I couldn't do anything but cry. Luke had died. My dad had disappeared, and I'd suffered a miscarriage. My hormones were all over the place. I didn't trust anyone and I didn't want to be around anyone. I needed to be safe and I needed to be alone.

I decided I had to leave James. He was too good and too nice and he'd gotten too close. I couldn't take the thought of any more loss. I wasn't worthy nor capable of loving anyone or anything but Logan.

I didn't deserve James and that was that.

"You can't leave me," James said, devastated by my sudden pronouncement that our marriage was over.

It was hard to blame him, given that I'd made the decision out of the blue one day and told him the next. Within a few days, I'd already rented a house on the ocean side of the beach and had a plan in place. As he left for his office in Irvine that morning, the movers were literally on their way over. I took Logan to school and the movers pulled up. I took everything I wanted and moved out of the house while he was at work.

James was legitimately furious, but I didn't budge. Eventually, he accepted that it was over between us, and got our marriage annulled since we had only been married nine months. His only real ask was that he be able to remain in Logan's life.

"Of course," I said and set up what turned out to be a very amicable visitation schedule. Later on, James legally adopted him.

I was, and am, forever grateful for his commitment to my, our, son.

# PHONE RECORD

Over the next year, people reported seeing my dad everywhere from the fake Las Vegas sighting to the Baskin Robbins in Laguna. He was supposedly spotted driving a Blue Mercedes or playing golf at a course near the Ritz-Carlton. I'd literally chase cars down on the freeway using techniques he taught me. I'd be in a restaurant in the middle of Arizona or New Mexico and think I saw him. I'd go into my house and see something had been moved. I'm very fanatical about detail and I know where everything is or is supposed to be. I was sure he'd broken into our house to check things out and moved some item just to "let me know" he was still watching me. He was always creepy and loved to spy on people, so it wasn't all that crazy a thought on my part. Then again, when someone's missing, you don't have any closure, so you're constantly looking, hoping to see them again.

My Aunt Sherri died in 1995 and I thought my Dad would come out of hiding for her funeral. I kept looking to see if he was watching from afar. Even my Aunt Brooke said, "I wonder if John Brown will come waltzing in and everyone will gasp at the funeral."

In 1996, two years after Dad disappeared, I was hanging out with Jason at his house in Corona del Mar. We were our usual tickling, punching, pushing selves. In fact, we were wrestling. He tossed me onto the bed, and I said something smartass to him.

"Don't talk to me like that," he said.

"I'll say whatever I want to say," I said.

We continued to scrap with each other until I fell off the bed.

As I was getting back up, I happened to look below the mattress and box spring and spotted a built-in car phone, the type installed in the center console between the front seats of cars in the 1990s. It wasn't just a random phone he'd gotten somewhere, but *the* phone that was in the Infiniti Q45 that had disappeared with my dad. I knew because I had been in Dad's Q45 many times.

Dad was missing. The car he'd been driving was missing, but his car phone was under my brother's bed? Jason would take anything of value off of cars. Jason had stripped the scooter he stole, taken all the parts, and put them on Carrie's. He knew how to strip license plates, scratch off VIN numbers. Dad had taught both boys to take anything of value and a car phone had value. Clearly, he'd seen the car just before or after my father's disappearance.

I wanted to say something when I saw the phone under the bed, but I knew that if I did, it was just going to cause a big problem. I was also scared of what I'd hear. I desperately wanted to believe that meant my father did come to Jason and tell them that if he disappeared to get rid of his stuff in twenty-four hours. The idea that maybe my brother did help him made that much more sense. Unfortunately, the other option—that he'd gotten rid of my dad— made equally as much sense. He didn't seem to care that dad had disappeared, nor shown any emotion as he tossed Dad's clothes in the trash can. I also noticed that after Dad was gone, he changed. When we watched movies or went somewhere and there'd be something really sick or sad on the news, he would laugh.

"That's not even funny," I'd say, worried he'd crossed over some line where he just didn't feel anymore.

Three years after Dad went missing, the Infiniti was found in Mexico near the border town of Brownsville, Texas. I always felt it was staged. My dad didn't like anything about Mexico but the gambling, and only then in Tijuana. No matter what happened or where he went, Dad didn't return.

I knew I had to do everything in my power not to think about it. Like a shark, it was my survival instinct to keep moving forward.

# LAW OF ATTRACTION

I'd like to say I learned my lesson about falling in love at first sight, but my penchant for meeting flashy, handsome men and diving into instant tempestuous relationships was due to repeat itself over and over. In fact, it happened almost immediately as I was moving out of the house I'd shared with James.

"I saw you at our kids' school open house," said a handsome man in an SUV who'd stopped in front of my house. He introduced himself as Antonio. "Do you need any help?"

"I'm good," I said, even though I was on crutches from a tennis injury.

"Do you want to go out sometime?" he asked.

He was tall, dark, handsome, and older—just my type—but I was honestly dumbfounded by his asking me out, literally as I was leaving my marriage.

I told him NO. Narcissists love to be told no, it's all about the chase—the hunt. They are relentless and will not give up till they have conquered you.

A few days later I was at the bank, and Antonio was there.

"Did you get moved?" he asked.

Although I'd left James, I still needed and wanted approval from men—specifically a certain kind of man. Antonio, handsome, Italian,

JAMI D. BROWN MARTIN

and eighteen years older than me, was not only a knight in shining armor, but a dead-on ringer for a father figure. However, unlike my missing dad, he owned a multi-million dollar company and was very well respected in the community. He also had kids who were Logan's age.

We fell right into a serious relationship.

Antonio, every bit the father figure for a girl who'd just lost hers, was very generous. He bought me an endless supply of $1000 shoes, designer handbags, and expensive jewelry. He had a thing for The Black Iris florist in Laguna Beach. From day one, arrangements sometimes costing sometimes well over $500 would be at my doorstep when I got home. One arrangement was so huge, I couldn't even get it through the doorway of my house. Antonio was extravagant to the point of being over the top and I loved the attention. It was a familiar kind of attention, and there was even more of it than I'd gotten from my first husband, Luke.

Antonio and I were engaged five times over the next seventeen drama-filled years. We broke up and got back together on a regular basis. Unlike Luke, Antonio never hit me or harmed me physically, but he was incredibly controlling and a chronic womanizer (hence the gift-giving which was often because he'd done something wrong and had gotten caught).

He would lay out outfits, complete with shoes for me to wear for an event. If I gained a pound, I would be body-shamed. No matter how perfect I looked, it was never enough and I was always worried, insecure, and suspicious. One morning, I was leaving to play tennis and forgot my purse. I slowly crept inside the house to see what he was up to, half expecting to find him on a call with another woman. Instead, he was watching porn on television at 7:30 AM.

Furious, I either threw or smashed with a baseball bat every TV in the house. He didn't say a word. He just slowly walked around the house, closing all the windows so the neighbors wouldn't hear the commotion. Next, I went after his VHS porn stash in the hall closet, hidden in the way back. The trash man was elated when I pushed the entire box out for him on trash day and asked if he would like some porn videos. I watched as he drove away with the entire collection in the passenger seat of the garbage truck.

Weeks later, when Antonio asked where his porn was, I told him the trash man had it.

When Antonio got in trouble, he never really said or did anything to defend himself. Instead, he would act like a small boy who was in trouble, mumbling "sorry" under his breath.

He claimed he only dated other women while we were broken up, but at one point, I found a phone book in his closet with the names of at least twenty women he juggled. Each entry also noted their shoe and dress sizes, and more personal information so he could keep track of all them.

I went back to my house, grabbed a bottle of wine and two glasses, and called a girlfriend. We proceeded to drink and dial every single chick in the black book. When I introduced myself and told them who I was and why I was calling, some of them would say, "What an asshole! I am so sorry, Jami." Others freaked out at me and said, "Don't ever call me again, I love him." A few even said, "Tell me more!"

It was one of the most bizarre relationship situations I'd ever dealt with and led to one of our many breakups. Each time we split, he'd woo me back with promises and gifts. He'd start a fight or break up with me to go on another date. I moved in and out of his house over and over again.

Another break-up happened after one of the girls he dated while we were off started sending perfumed letters and threatening to kill me. We had to get a restraining order and go to court.

I was so naïve I truly thought I could fix him. When I convinced him to go to therapy, he played along. The therapist asked me to stay at the end of our first session. As Antonio left in his car, the therapist sat beside me to console me through my tears. Her words are so clear, I remember them like they happened yesterday: "RUN! Run as far away and as fast as you can."

"But, I love him," I said, ignoring her advice.

I truly didn't understand what a narcissist was and I believed his chronic infidelity meant there was something physically flawed about me. If I looked the part with perfectly manicured nails and toes, styled hair, and dressed the way he wanted me to as I entertained his friends and business associates in exactly the way he wanted me to, then he would be faithful and never leave. All along I thought it was me, I was not enough.

I was, of course, wrong.

Besides, we were both addicted to drama.

I began to do the opposite of what Antonio wanted, which created more drama. I would go to Beverly Hills for the day, drinking and shopping with a girlfriend. If I got back late, (after the curfew he set for me), he would gather up my belongings into black trash bags and heave them over his ocean view balcony. I would just sit on the side of his house with my girlfriend, smoke weed, and laugh together until he calmed down.

Once, we were on a road trip and he told me to turn off the CD that was playing. I didn't. So he did. I'd been happily singing along to the words, so I turned it back on. He reached over, turned it off, and in that deep scary voice he tried to use to intimidate me said, "NO MUSIC!"

When he wasn't looking, I tossed the black leather case with his entire CD collection out of the car and onto State Route 111, somewhere on the highway to Palm Springs.

He definitely wasn't happy the next day when he noticed they were gone.

It wouldn't be the last time. I also threw a $20,000 ring out the window. When he took me back after that fight, he asked me to marry him again.

I leaned on men like Antonio because I was taught I couldn't do it alone. I couldn't quite escape from believing a man would fix all my problems and make me safe and complete.

While we were definitely together but not living together, I let myself into his house, opened the door to his bedroom, and found him with a brunette flight attendant (who lived in L.A.) and her yapping little dogs in the bed.

I preceded to bark commands at the girl to get dressed and get out of the house. She wouldn't budge. Despite being completely naked, Antonio tried his best to defuse the situation between his girlfriend and the other woman. I'd had it with all these women and told her to get out, threatening her with Antonio's unloaded gun which I'd taken from his nightstand drawer. She called 911. I chucked the gun into the bushes as two sheriffs arrived and told Antonio to get dressed. He refused, so there we were in the living room, two

sheriffs, a naked man, two women fighting over him, and the yapping dogs.

The woman wouldn't leave because she had been drinking, so
Antonio left in the car with me. Halfway to my house, I threw him
out of my car. I just wanted to make it clear that his nonsense had
to stop.

Typical co-dependent that I was, I accepted his guilt gifts and his
assurances that it would never happen again. It would take years to
learn the only way to get away from him (or any narcissist) was to
move away—as far away as I could.

When Logan was in middle school, one of the now grown kids I used
to babysit for back on Hillview Drive overdosed. I was very affected
by his loss and donated my time to a non-profit in Laguna Beach
whenever I had a free moment. I really enjoyed serving the community and helping others whose lives mirrored my childhood.

I also enrolled at Saddleback College to get my drug and alcohol
counseling certification. I took a full load, finished early, and made
the Dean's List. In order to get the certification, I had to do internship hours and was hired, with pay, at Laguna Beach High School.
Given the wild, unruly life I'd led while there, it was ironic that I
ended up back where I started, but to help and heal.

I had my own classroom and was given the opportunity to help
kids like me who used drugs and alcohol to numb the pain. The
internship was short lived, less than a year, but I count it as one of
my most impactful accomplishments. Many of the teachers who'd

witnessed my rebellious nature but recognized my pain and helped me regardless were still at the school. Even the Dean of Students was still there but working as an English teacher. (She would go on to teach Logan when he entered high school.) I told her she was the reason I stayed in high school. She told me I made her proud and made her see the difference she'd made by being there for me and pushing me along.

Between one of my many breakups with Antonio, James sold his dot-com business and told me he wanted to celebrate by taking Logan on a series of trips to see the world. We were on good terms and James kindly invited me to come along, all expenses paid, even offering to book me my own room so I could share the experience with my son. We spent the better part of a year taking trips together to Australia, Japan, Europe, and all over China. I even helped him with a business in Taipei. On one of the last trips, which was to the Caribbean, we fell back in love.

After eight years of being apart, we reunited for nearly two years.

Jason would often come to visit when I was back together with James. I was not home one particular afternoon when Jason pulled out a black briefcase.

"What is that?" James asked.

Jason opened up the black briefcase (which was eerily similar to the Magic Bag John Brown had) and neatly laid stacks of money and three passports on the counter— one blue, one red, and one green.

"What is all that for?" James asked.

"You have to be ready, you never know when you just need to go," Jason said.

James never mentioned it to me at the time. He figured it was just typical bizarre Brown behavior.

He only wishes now that he'd noted the actual names on the passports.

During that time, I enrolled in an interior design school in Newport Beach. It was private and expensive and James didn't hesitate to pay the tuition.

While other students graduated and went off to work for large commercial and residential design firms, I started with James's house, paying him back for putting me through school with a complete redesign and renovation. I gutted his place down to the studs and redesigned everything—new floorplan, walls, furniture, fixtures, and finishing touches. I even re-landscaped the pool and surrounding yard, repainted the exterior, and took one of the side garages and put in an 18-piece gym. When he sold the house a few years later, he made a hefty profit.

A friend from high school whose husband was affiliated with partners who owned the land where the Montage is located in Laguna Beach asked me if I'd redesign her house. I did and she loved my work. Word spread. I quickly built a portfolio, made some business cards, got a business license, and started JD Martin Design.

It was all word of mouth and the work rolled in.

Soon after, I was on the "A" list, designing house after house along the coast. I was hired by a real estate developer to do a renovation on his residence—one of fourteen situated along Emerald Bay. The owners bought the home for approximately twelve million dollars.

After renovations, the four story, 9,000 square foot home, known as "Cresting Wave," featured curving copper roofs, a glass-covered 64-foot gallery along the upper, stone-paved floor, and a spiral stairway encircling a cylindrical glass elevator topped with a conical skylight. It was later resold in 2009 for 34.5 million dollars, the second priciest residential property in Orange County.

During that time, I'd gone from living in James's guest house to moving back into the main house with him. We talked about remarrying, but when things got too serious or too comfortable, I got anxious. It was my sign to leave before anyone could leave me.

Unlike the last time I'd abandoned James, however, I left everything in the house, including the keys to the Mercedes I'd been driving. I took a taxi to the BMW dealership and moved on to my next chapter.

James, who was better prepared for my inability to commit, continued to raise Logan as his own. He drove him to all his basketball tournaments, paid for his private coaching, and gave him the best of the best. When I moved to Santa Margarita so Logan could establish residency to play basketball, James moved out of his place in Laguna and rented a place near us for Logan's sake.

I consider James a great blessing and Logan does too.

# THE GAME OF LIFE

On his Wikipedia page, it says that Jason owned Toys Unlimited. Jason had taken out a DBA while living in Utah called Toys Unlimited, but he was definitely not a toy salesman. I told the FBI that Jason had a lot of toys, meaning boats, cars, and ATVs and someone turned that fact around—the true details of Jason's life get jumbled frequently. The FBI said that Jason also started up a modeling agency with his friend, mainly to hook up with the girls. Apparently, they charged $500 to take photos of aspiring models and potential clients had begun to report Picture Perfect Modeling to the Better Business Bureau as a scam.

That I believe.

I also read a somewhere that Jason, "took pains to project himself as a fun-loving surfer dude with a golden touch for business – as a schemer who became addicted to an expensive, showy lifestyle of drugs, gambling, $500 bar tabs, strippers and partiers, scam busi-nesses, and expensive vehicles." He definitely gambled and must have run his usual check and bank fraud scams to finance his big spending.

On the Doorstep Advertising, another one of the businesses Jason supposedly co-owned with Brad was theoretically part of the golf business. Like Dad, Jason was an amazing golfer and would make money on the golf course. He and Brad did go to golf courses with a plan to sign them up with the marketing company they'd created and, of course, play the course for free. Brad had always been quiet. He wasn't flashy or showy. His wife had a job and he watched the kids and tried to get businesses off the ground. Jason, however, was inherently lazy.

In January 2000, Jason and a friend walked into Under Par golf shop in Reidsville, North Carolina. While his friend was chatting up the owner, Jason walked out with three pricey golf clubs and added it to their "import" inventory.

As they drove on to another shop called Tee to Green in Eden, North Carolina, the owner called the police. By the time the sales-clerk was alerted to be on the lookout for two handsome, nicely dressed men in their early thirties driving a brown car with Florida plates, they'd already left with whatever Jason had lifted.

Officers spotted the car and pulled Jason over. In the trunk were the stolen clubs. Jason and his friend produced IDs, not theirs of course. Both were handcuffed, taken in, fingerprinted, and put in a holding cell. Jason's prints hit on prior charges, leading officers to their real names. While the clubs were returned and Jason got away with only a misdemeanor theft charge, a story about the incident appeared in an article in *Golf Digest* by Dave Kindred:

*As robberies go, it was minor-league stuff.*

*The blond dude simply walked out of a golf shop with three titanium drivers. He could not have been much more obvious. When you run a golf store in the north of North Carolina and it's January, you notice a* guy who comes in wearing loafers and no socks, especially if his ankles are tanned. Here's what you think: Dude's not from around here.

So Pete Hare, who owned the Under Par store on Freeway Road in Reidsville, noticed No Socks. The man wandered around the store while his buddy talked to Hare about putting. Theft is an occupational hazard in golf stores. It's easy to slip out with a dozen golf balls. It's more difficult to shoplift three drivers, though it happens often enough that store owners will tell you, "He put 'em down his pants."

On that day in January 2000, soon after the strangers left, Hare took a look around. Yep, down the dude's pants: three drivers, maybe $299 each.

Hare alerted a friend, Jerry Woodall, who ran a golf store a few miles north. "Be on the lookout for a couple thieves," Hare said.

"They've already been here and left," Woodall said. "Headed back your way."

A phone call did it. No bloodhounds were necessary. The thieves were stopped along Highway 14, north of Reidsville. One imagines Barney Fife at work. The small-time collar became a big-time deal.

# PHOENIX

In May 2003 Jason moved from Salt Lake City to Phoenix. He loved warm weather and wanted to be closer to Lake Havasu. Jason, being Jason, instantly charmed, and began to date the attractive realtor who had showed him the house he rented on Nighthawk Way in the Ahwatukee Foothills. She just happened to live next door.

She thought of Jason as cute, fit, and full of boyish charm. He said he ran a golf import-export business with his brother and needed garage space more than anything to store his gear. He moved in with nice furniture as well as his golf equipment, bikes, a motorcycle, jet skis, quads, and the cars—a new black Escalade, a Jeep Rubicon, and a silver M-series BMW convertible. He put his Master Craft wakeboard boat into a nearby storage unit. All the neighbors liked him and said he was friendly, fun, athletic, and always out on the street skateboarding.

Jason loved to have a good time and shared his "fun" with everyone. He took his neighbor and her son waterskiing and to Diamondback games. Whenever we visited Jason, no matter where he was living, he took Logan to do all kinds of things. We called it Camp Uncle Jason in the summertime because Jason would come and get Logan and they'd go boating and wakeboarding at Lake Havasu, or camping, fishing, and off to ride ATVs. Logan had the time of his life with his uncle.

In typical fashion, Jason always seemed to have loads of cash on him and was very generous, spending hundreds a night out on the town with pals. An anonymous ex later told the Phoenix police that Jason gave her $5000 for breast implants and had done the same for another girlfriend.

Jason had inherited his own version of my now missing father's obsessive-compulsive personality. When he did something, it was always to the extreme. If he was going to start working out, he did it hours a day. If he was going to have toys to play with, he was going to have all the toys. Everything was always meticulous, in order, clean, and neat.

Around the time of his golf club arrest, Jason was living in Salt Lake City. I came into town for a visit and remember finding water bottles that were partially filled with blue liquid that looked like mouthwash or Windex. They were in his car, in the sofa cushions, and even in his kitchen. Once, when he came to California, my cleaning lady found a couple of bottles and put them under my sink. I found it weird, but given Jason's OCD streak, I wasn't surprised by much.

As it turned out, Jason was addicted to something called GHB—or gamma-hydroxybutyric acid—a blue liquid that bodybuilders used to increase production of human growth hormone (HGH) and gave them a feeling of well-being that enabled them to lift heavier weights. A capful gave people a feeling of being super-human and invincible.

GHB which is produced naturally in small amounts by the body and sold on the street under names like Easy Lay, G, Georgia Home Boy, Goop, Grievous Bodily Harm, Liquid Ecstasy, Liquid X, and Scoop provided the euphoric feeling of alcohol without the side effects. Because GHB caused a coma-like sleep in high doses, especially when mixed with alcohol, it is more widely known as the date-rape drug. The FDA banned it as a Schedule I substance alongside heroin and LSD in 2001.

Brad told me after the fact that Jason was addicted and had been hospitalized twice for an overdose. Given his OCD nature and the effects of GHB, I'm not surprised he'd been struggling.

Within six months of living in Phoenix, Jason told his neighbors-turned-friends he had to leave because his sister-in-law had breast cancer, and he needed to go back to California to run both his and his brother's end of the business while she sought treatment. Brad's wife was perfectly healthy at the time. He also mentioned that Brad had been complaining he was "sick and tired" of him spending money trying to develop new clients in Arizona.

I had no idea that Jason had moved out and put all of his stuff in storage, or that he was having any issues. All I did notice was that he'd become distant. We used to talk on the phone all the time, but suddenly it stopped. During the year before the murder, I hardly saw or heard from him. It never occurred to me that Jason couldn't make his rent and that he was basically living at campgrounds with his best friend, using the bathroom and laundry facilities there, while he was figuring out where to go.

Brad later told me, "He's been in such a dark place. I've been giving him money and he calls me on the phone all wasted saying he doesn't want to live anymore and he screwed his life up."

The last time I saw Jason, he told me that the guy who he was buying the GHB from was killed.

"How did he die?" I asked.

"He jumped out in front of an eighteen-wheeler truck and tried to stop it."

I truly believe his addiction to GHB was responsible, at least in part, for his emotional decline and any criminal delusions he may have harbored.

# TARGET PRACTICE

Jason bought a .45 caliber Glock and high-powered rounds from Totally Awesome Guns and Range in Salt Lake City, Utah, two weeks before the murder of armed guard, Keith Palomares, outside of the AMC theater in Ahwatukee. The owner of the gun store, Clark Aposhian, not only sold Jason a .45 caliber Glock semiautomatic handgun, but two boxes of Corbon Pow'R Ball hollow-point bullets, a box of another type of ammo, two practice targets, and a range pass. He ran a background check which showed him to be clear of domestic charges and felonies and took Jason's fingerprints. Jason insisted he be enrolled in the class to learn how to shoot the Glock that day. Clark Aposhian described Jason as looking like a "surfer dude" and as an "arrogant cocky little shit" who didn't know how to handle a pistol.

By the end of the four hour class, Jason's aim had improved so much, he was hitting a small cluster on the targets within an inch and a half from his intended spot. Clark Aposhian said that nothing about my brother struck him as suspicious or dangerous.

A year after he moved out of the house in Phoenix two weeks before Thanksgiving, Jason called the realtor he'd dated and asked if he could stay with her for a few days while he was in town on business. Still friends, she was glad to have him in her home.

He arrived in the silver BMW with a large duffel, a dop kit, clothes on hangers, and his own pillow and towel. No longer romantically involved, he stayed on the sofa which he tidied up every morning before he left for the day to "meet with clients."

In other words, he was a model guest.

In the days leading up to Thanksgiving, employees in the strip mall businesses surrounding the AMC reported noticing a silver BMW with tinted windows in the parking lot. The driver, male and always alone, sat there for hours with the motor running. He talked on his cell phone and was seen writing on a notepad. He never got out of the car and no one ever approached. Each day, he parked in a different space, but would change locations multiple times throughout the morning. Apparently, he went into the coffee shop on the courtyard in front of the theater at one point and asked a barista a few questions about the timing of the armored car.

My brother may have been lazy, but he was definitely precise and planned the things he did do carefully.

The day before Thanksgiving, Jason left the realtor's home saying his business in Phoenix was finished.

From her place, Jason checked into room 261 at the Extended Stay America at the intersection of I-10 and East Chandler Blvd—less than two miles from the AMC theater in Ahwatukee. He used a credit card to pay for four nights, giving his home address as 2546 Dearborn Street, Salt Lake City, Utah—which was where he lived before moving to Phoenix. He described his car as a silver, two door BMW and crossed out his license number on the form. He immediately put the do not disturb sign on his door and left it there for the entirety of his stay.

On Sunday, November 28, 2004, three days after Thanksgiving, Jason went out to the middle of the Tonto National Forest northeast of Phoenix and set up paper plates in the scrub brush for some target practice.

On that day, a local man named Max Newton was wrapping up a weekend camping trip with some friends and his ten-year-old son. They were packing up to go when they heard gunfire. Suddenly bullets grazed past them and hit the driver's side door of his SUV.

"Stop shooting!" Max Newton shouted. "There are people up here!"

The shooting stopped instantly.

Max climbed onto his ATV, rode down to where the firing came from, and found Jason standing alone. His BMW was parked nearby.

"What in the hell are you doing shooting out here?" he asked. "I've got kids over there, and you just shot holes in my car."

"I'm so sorry!" Jason said. "I had no idea anyone else was around."

Jason got in his car and followed Max Newton back to the campground area to assess the damage he'd caused. When he saw the holes in the door of the man's 1999 Ford F250 pickup, Jason took a spare paper plate from his front seat and wrote his contact info which included the Dearborn address in Salt Lake City and a phone number with a Texas area code. He signed the plate and told Max Newton to call him with an estimate.

Before they parted ways, Max Newton asked Jason what kind of gun he had.

Jason showed him the .45 Glock.

# MONDAY, NOVEMBER 29, 2004

There have been many articles and television shows devoted to Jason Brown and the events that occurred before, during, and after Monday, November 29th, 2004, but research done by Paige Williams for her now out-of-print book, *The Ghost*, provided the best corroboration of what I've been able to piece together over the years:

On Monday morning, November 29, 2004, Max Newton got a damage estimate of $1300. He called Jason just before 10:00 AM but got voice mail and left no message. At the same time, the staff of the AMC Ahwatukee 24 theater at Ray Road and 50th Street were preparing to open for the day. Keith Palomares and his partner arrived in front of the theater in a Dunbar armored car, like they did every Monday. Palomares got out of the truck with his sidearm holstered and the pouch unclipped. He walked into the courtyard toward the theater holding the duffel bag he would use to transport the weekend receipts back to the truck.

He reached the glass front doors and a manager came to let him in. Per AMC regulations, a second employee joined them and they proceeded together to the safe. Palomares held a Dunbar key, which accessed the safe's combination lock. The manager opened the safe to thirteen plastic bank bags, sealed and numbered, each containing various amounts of currency, almost all of it in bills. Typical Monday deposits totaled around $20,000, but it was the weekend after Thanksgiving which is a traditionally busy moviegoing weekend and there was a total of $56,039.07 in the safe. Palomares did all the necessary paperwork and stowed the money in the duffel. By training, the process had to be completed in less than seven minutes. He completed the transaction in less than four.

For most of the morning, painters who were working outside one of the nearby stores noticed a man in dark clothes and sunglasses standing around the edges of the courtyard with his arms folded. A black and red mountain bike was leaned against the wall beside an access alley. One of the painters was headed to spit out his gum when he saw the man step out of the breezeway. As Palomares exited the doors of the theater into the courtyard holding the movie and concession receipts, the shooter pulled out a .45 caliber handgun and ambushed the guard.

One hollow point bullet shattered the window of the box office.

The other five went point blank into Palomares's head, assassination style.

Palomares's partner, who was back in the armored truck, heard the gunshots and thought someone was banging on the side. He checked his mirrors but couldn't see anything. He pulled forward and saw a man standing over his partner, pulling at the money duffel. Because Dunbar drivers are trained to remain with their vehicle at all times, he could only call in the emergency and wait for his supervisor to arrive.

The shooter hopped on the bike he'd stashed next to the theater and took off.

From the courtyard, one of the painters yelled at him to stop. He did stop for the briefest of seconds, turned around and looked at the painter, then vanished around the corner.

To this day, I struggle to believe my brother could really be the shooter in question, but there were nearly two dozen witnesses—the Dunbar driver, the bench painters, coffee shop employees, maintenance workers, janitors, movie theater staff, a cleaning crew coming off the graveyard shift, and even a plumber retrieving a hand snake from his truck. Most reported seeing a man in black jeans, a dark hooded sweatshirt, and sunglasses hanging out in the east breezeway, as if waiting for someone. There was general agreement that he disappeared down the alley, carrying a bag, on a black and red mountain bike. A motorist saw a man pedaling fast southbound on South 50th Street toward an office park. The killer was described as white or Hispanic. Some said brown hair, some said blond. One thought he'd seen a mustache and long sideburns. One remembered a goatee.

As Phoenix law enforcement and the FBI were getting the call and beginning to converge on Ahwatukee Foothills, the cell phones registered to Jason one in Utah the other in Texas were getting and making lot of calls.

10:05 AM: Jason called Brad and said he was in Arizona with his friend and that he needed to get to a 24-Hour Fitness to meet a girl.

Brad was shopping at Home Depot and told him he'd call him back when he got home and could go online to look up the closest gym. Before he could, Jason called back and said he'd found the place and was on the treadmill.

Apparently, 59 calls were made or received between 10:05 AM and 10:48 AM, 34 of them between Jason and Brad. Brad would later tell authorities they were just chatting about "women and stuff" and that Jason never mentioned the murder or the robbery. Jason does appear on the gym's security video taken later that day. The cameras show him taking a duffel bag inside, leaving without it, and returning later to pick it up.

11:25 AM: Jason called the Extended Stay just ahead of his noon check-out time and said he wanted to stay anther night. The clerk asked him to wait while she ran the credit card on file. She reported that he seemed impatient, repeatedly asking, "Can I go now?" and, "Is that it?" over what sounded like traffic noises in the background.

Max Newton tried to call again and didn't leave a message.

2:17 PM: There was a call to Greyhound.

2:21PM: There was another call to Greyhound.

5:02 PM: There was a call from a creditor.

Twenty uniformed patrol officers, fifteen police detectives, six FBI agents, five police sergeants, one lieutenant, nine civilian techs and trainees, and a SWAT unit with dogs converged on the scene. Among them were police detective Tom Kulesa and FBI special agent Lance Leising who was six years out of the FBI and working lead on the case. Forensic photographers took 253 color shots, including aerials. The theater turned over seven days' worth of surveillance tapes and gave investigators the first look at a man in black who was ducking in and out of the breezeway in the moments before the shooting. At 10:00 AM, the figure popped out and moved toward the theater. The footage next showed him moving back into the breezeway with a duffel. He was of average height, anywhere from mid-twenties to mid-forties, either white or Hispanic, wearing dark clothing and sunglasses and riding a bike.

Air patrol spotted an abandoned red and black mountain bike on the other side of 50th Street in a drainage area behind shrubs and mesquite. Techs began processing it for fingerprints. The prints would match the set Clark Aposhian took from Jason when he sold him both the gun and the ammo back in Utah, as well as those for the golf shop arrest in North Carolina. Surveillance cameras at 24-Hour Fitness showed a man fitting Jason's appearance entering at 4:23 PM. At 5:30 PM, cameras showed him walking around the gym and then leaving without the duffel. At 7:03 PM, he returned then he walked out a few mins later, once again carrying the duffel.

The clerk at the Extended Stay didn't see or hear from Jason again until just after 6:00 PM, when he entered the lobby dressed casually in shorts and a t-shirt and looking to have his card re-keyed. A few minutes later, a white guy, about thirty, who was tall and slender with dark hair showed up as well. He and Jason chatted for a moment and then they both left simultaneously, or together. The clerk wasn't sure.

Within the hour, another Extended Stay guest who'd been living at the hotel came in to report that he had seen the man from room 261 loading his belongings including a black and red duffel on wheels, clothes on hangers, and some other belongings into a silver BMW with Utah plates. It seemed weird to him because the man wouldn't make eye contact.

The clerk asked for the plate number. When the guy went to get it, the BMW was gone. The clerk called in to report a suspicious person but couldn't let police into room 261 because he hadn't checked out and wasn't going to until the next day. All she could do was re-program the door so that if he returned, he'd have to get a new key and she could discretely call the police.

He didn't return.

Max Newton dialed Jason again just before 8:00 PM. Jason, who was driving toward Henderson, Nevada where he would spend the night, answered. He was courteous, remorseful, and felt terrible about damaging the truck. Newton gave him the estimate and was told he'd receive a check in the mail soon. Newton said he'd hang onto the bullet. Jason said his brother had been all over him about being stupid enough to shoot without a backstop and asked him to, "Let it lie."

A week later, Max Newton still hadn't received a check, so he called again and left a message on Monday evening December 6, 2004. At that time, the Phoenix police had just released the identity of the Dunbar Armored murder suspect along with a photo. Not long after hanging up, Newton saw the news and thought, that the guy kind of looked like Sean Penn and tried to place where he'd seen him. When he heard thirty-five years old and Salt Lake City, he fetched the paper plate with the writing on it and saw that everything matched down to the license plate number.

Freaked out, he called the police.

The next day when Max Newton got home from work, he found a letter in the mail with an apology from Jason along with a certified check for $1300. He also included a Toys R Us gift certificate for Newton's son.

The dichotomy of it all just blows my mind.

# ESCALADE ESCAPADE

The police and FBI knew that a man matching Jason's description, and driving a silver BMW M3 convertible had been staying at the Extended Stay hotel in Chandler, Arizona. He'd checked in on November 25, 2004 and left abruptly the evening of the crime. A fingerprint lifted from the BMX bike matched Jason's prints, and police found out that he recently bought a Glock .45 caliber gun and ammunition, which matched the weapon used in the murder.

On November 30, 2004, Jason made a bank deposit in Henderson, Nevada. From there, he went to his storage unit he kept in the Las Vegas area, parked the BMW, and swapped it out for his Escalade. He then drove to Brad's house. The next morning, Jason made another deposit at the Union Bank branch in Dana Point and went golfing with Brad. Afterwards, they went shooting at an indoor firing range. Jason took his .45 caliber Glock and Brad shot his 9-millimeter. They also rented a .40 caliber Glock. They bought ammunition for all three, although Jason already had bullets for his Glock. As soon as they were done at the range, Jason called me, and then rolled up in the Escalade for his week-long surprise visit.

❖ ❖ ❖

On December 4, 2004, the Maricopa Superior Court issued a warrant for Jason's arrest. He was charged with first degree murder, robbery, and unlawful flight. Phoenix Police Department case number 2004-42261950 would quickly grow to more than 200 pages.

The Phoenix police department wanted to have a press conference to inform the public that a fugitive was at large, but FBI special agent Lance Leising wanted to keep Jason's identity quiet for fear of tipping him off. While the police believed Jason was armed and dangerous, and his name needed to be released for public safety, Leising correctly surmised that Jason was back in the Laguna area and he needed time to get California agents in place. Leising was able to stall the local police for twenty-four hours before my brother's image began to flood the airwaves.

When the realtor saw Jason's photo on television, she assumed the police had the wrong person and called to let my brother know so the mistake could be corrected. On December 6, 2004, Brad got a voicemail from a Phoenix reporter trying to track down relatives of Jason Brown. He called Jason immediately.

"Why are reporters looking to talk to me about you?" Brad asked.

"You need to meet me right now," Jason said.

Jason dropped Logan off at school for me that morning and then met Brad at his office. To this day, I have never heard much about what was said other than Jason apparently told Brad that he didn't want to get him involved in this.

Jason then came to my house, collected his things, and took off.

I was unaware that the authorities had begun contacting our extended family, and that my cousin, who'd held a grudge against Jason for stealing her wedding gifts and hiding them in the attic crawl space above where my dad was living, gave the authorities my home address.

I don't know what I would have done had I known the FBI would be raiding my house within hours.

At the very least, I would have gotten Logan the hell out of there.

# CAT AND MOUSE

Jason disappeared and I was left devastated and in shock with the media parked outside of my house and the phone ringing non-stop. When I turned on the TV, I saw a photo of my brother on the news, *Nancy Grace*, and a half dozen other programs. The Brown family façade had not cracked but was being analyzed daily. Worse, I was a focal point because I was the last person to see my brother.

All I could think was, *this can't be happening...*

Even though the evidence overwhelmingly pointed to Jason, there was a part of me that wanted to believe he could be innocent. I couldn't believe that he had killed another human being. And for what? $50,000 dollars? I'd seen him burn through that much money in a month. Was he so messed up on GHB that he didn't know what he was doing? Was he that desperate? The Jason I thought I knew was much smarter than that. If he were going to rob an armored vehicle, he'd at least rob one that just left a bank so he could get a million or two million dollars. Why a movie theater? What if the guy only had $10,000 in his bag? How could my brother be a murderer?

Jason may have conned a lot of people, but always came to me when stuff wasn't going right. I'm good at reading people. I can tell when something's wrong. I can tell if someone is lying to me. And yet, I completely missed what was going on with him. I assume he thought he was going to get away with what he did because when he came to California to see me, he truly acted like everything was fine.

In the aftermath, I was anything but fine. I couldn't trust anyone because I didn't know who might say what to the FBI. Would I go to go to jail? What was going to happen with my life? I would literally lay on the floor and sob for hours. It was unfathomable that Jason could have committed such a violent act. How was it even possible that he had vanished just like my father, ten years earlier?

Everyone in the Mormon community from Newport Beach to Salt Lake City heard about the former missionary who'd been accused of murder. As I was in gut-wrenching, soul searing pain, the authorities were getting numerous calls, tips, and information: Jason had been blacklisted at Nordstrom for shoplifting, his house in Salt Lake City had a weird home office that was off-limits to his roommates, he and another man named Jason claimed that they dealt GHB together in Las Vegas. He said Jason came through town a few days before the murder complaining he hated staying on people's couches and that he, "didn't want to live like that anymore."

He claims Jason also told him, "I'm going to go get me some money," and asked the other Jason if he wanted in.

The other Jason thought it sounded crazy and didn't believe any of it was for real.

Meanwhile, I was stuck with the reality of it all, living a nightmare but unable to sleep. On the one hand, I'd changed all my numbers literally the day after I met with the FBI at Antonio's office. I did not want to take the chance that Jason could convince me to help him and drag me further into the hell he'd created. On the other, I did little else but pray for some kind of information that might allow me to believe my brother had somehow been subjected to a horrible case of mistaken identity.

And then, Brad and I were called and told to meet the FBI at the Laguna post office.

My dad always taught us to have post office boxes. He always said, "Nobody but you can go open your mailbox. It's safe."

Jason knew both Brad and I kept a post office box in Laguna. Inside Brad's P.O. box was a package from Jason. It was postmarked San Diego.

"He's in San Diego," the agents barked into their phones. "He's headed to Mexico."

*Jason hates Mexico,* I thought but didn't say as the authorities instructed us to follow them to the police station, which was four doors down from the post office. Once inside the interrogation room, we were instructed to open the box. As it turned out, my dad was technically right that the FBI couldn't open our mail, but they could certainly root through it all with us present. We could only watch as they put on latex gloves and removed the contents which included Jason's Texas cell phone, his hoodies, and a 24-Hour Fitness card in the name of Brad's business. Brad's 9-millimeter handgun, which Brad said he must have stolen from his garage, was also in the box.

"Do you think he's with your father in Mexico?" I was asked.

"No way," I said, just as I'd said on the day after Jason disappeared when Special Agent Leising interviewed me. Also seated at the conference table that day in Antonio's office with the handful of FBI agents was the detective who'd interviewed me ten years earlier about my dad's disappearance. He was still determined to solve his disappearance.

"Remember me?" he asked.

"How could I forget," I managed.

"When I saw your brother on the news, I ran to the files. His case has never left my mind. I can't believe both of them are missing?"

"Me either," I said.

"So shocking."

At that point, I could barely force myself to nod.

Brad said as little as possible, simply calling Jason lazy and a gambler who loved to take risks.

As I predicted, Jason didn't gamble his way down to Mexico like the authorities continued to suspect. He'd mailed the package from San Diego and then immediately headed north. Knowing they were looking for a silver BMW and probably saying, "Thanks Jami," he cruised up the 101 to Oregon in his tricked out Escalade with 22 inch rims, Play Station, TVs behind the seats, and blacked out windows, keeping track of the news and aware the FBI were down in San Diego looking for him. A week later, Jason mailed Brad another package from Oregon.

When the FBI insisted we meet them at the post office again, we said, "We want gloves. We want to go through the stuff ourselves."

"It's evidence. You can't touch anything!" they said.

In the second package was a laptop, the rest of Jason's IDs, his ski passes, photographs, and a ninety minute video of him boating at Lake Havasu. The FBI took all the videos, photographs, and CDs with photos on them. They remain in evidence.

The task force, which had mistakenly headed south, now turned north but they didn't find Jason. On January 18, 2005, four weeks after he'd gone missing, the Escalade was found in the long-term parking at the international terminal of the Portland airport.

Finally, Jason had made a move that made sense to me. Dad used to leave cars in long term parking when he was trying to hide them. We all knew you could leave a car in long-term parking at any airport for thirty days before they'd tag and tow you. The Escalade's windows had been broken out and the GPS that was built into the console had been ripped out. The FBI believed Jason broke his own windows to make the car look stolen and then caught a plane overseas. That, or he got a hold of another car and drove up to Canada to make permanent use of his French. Another theory had him trading vehicles with someone in San Diego near the border so he could keep going south while whoever that someone was drove his Escalade back, mailed his packages and, then got on a plane headed wherever. I thought that Jason could have hopped a freighter on the Oregon coast. Jason likely left Oregon, but he wouldn't have been able to get on a plane with his passports because all of the aliases he used were being monitored. Besides, if he was going to get on a plane, he'd have done it immediately after he allegedly robbed the movie theater back in Arizona.

Wherever he was, Jason had clearly planned to throw the FBI off and set them on a different trail. He'd mailed the first package from San Diego so the FBI would look for him there, giving him time to drive up the coast where he mailed another package. By hiding the car in long-term parking he had another thirty days to vanish.

And then he was gone.

# STORAGE LOCKER

There was one question the authorities kept asking me from the very beginning:

"Where is Jason's BMW?"

"I don't know," I told them. "I do know Jason has a storage unit somewhere."

"Where?"

"I think it's in Arizona. He has a house in Arizona, too."

The first time I was told there was no house in Arizona, and that he was couch surfing and living in camping grounds with his friend for the past year, I was dumbfounded. The day he left, Jason had told me he was headed back to his house in Arizona because of the sprinkler issue. The last time I'd visited him, I'd stayed at that house. It wasn't until later that Brad told me how depressed and broke Jason had been over the past year, and that he'd lent him thousands of dollars just to stay afloat. Still, it was hard to imagine Jason moving from campground to campground, even with his good buddy.

The FBI continued to press me. "We need to find the vehicle that was used in the murder."

"I don't know where it is," I said, "I do know Brad mentioned something about a storage unit in Las Vegas."

The FBI went right back to Brad.

"Where's the storage unit in Las Vegas?" they asked him.

"There is no storage unit in Las Vegas," he said.

Because the storage unit was actually in Henderson just outside of Las Vegas, Brad figured he wasn't technically lying.

He got into his Suburban, drove to Laguna Canyon and hired some day laborers, and drove to Las Vegas in the middle of the night. Using a key Jason must have given him during their last meeting, Brad emptied out Jason's storage unit and took the contents back to his house.

As I connected the dots, I figured that Jason owed Brad money so he must have given him the storage unit keys and said, "Here, take it all for the money I owe you."

The FBI had alerted all the storage businesses in the area to be on the lookout, so when the owner saw the contents of Jason's locker being emptied, including ATVs, a boat, and a silver 2003 BMW M3 (which Brad had one of the day laborers drive back to California) he called the authorities.

The FBI just missed Brad, passing him on an off-ramp.

The first thing Brad did when he got back home was to have the BMW washed and detailed. Brad was a neat freak and was only washing the car because it was dirty, not thinking he was washing away prints. Brad took the clean, now fingerprint-free car Jason used in the armed car robbery and hid it from the FBI by putting it in his storage unit.

The FBI asked him several times, "Where's the BMW?"

Brad tried to wait them out by failing to return their phone calls or answering the door.

Brad let me know he'd cleaned out Jason's storage units and brought everything back. I told one of the officers who called me that Brad had it in another storage locker.

A week later, I got another call from the FBI. "We just need to know where the BMW is."

"I told someone that Brad has the BMW over a week ago," I said.

For whatever reason, the officer who had called me the week before hadn't relayed the message, had misunderstood me, or who knows what happened, and they were shocked to hear that bit of information.

On Friday, April 9, 2005, the FBI rushed Brad's house by hopping over the large high retaining wall that surrounded his property, once again, in the most dramatic, traumatic way possible. Brad spotted them from inside and headed down the hall to call his attorney. He then called me. I could hear the screaming and Brad being wrestled to the ground by federal agents yelling commands. Thinking he was trying to flee, they shattered his custom glass entry door, handcuffed him, and dragged him out of the house in front of his three small children.

As soon as I heard what had happened, I jumped in my car and headed over to his place. I arrived to the completely heartbreaking sight of his four-year-old son trying to clean up the glass with a little broom and dustpan. While his wife dealt with his arrest, I made the kids dinner, helped them with their homework, and took care of them, trying to make things seem as normal as possible.

Unfortunately, the days of normal were long over for all of us.

Brad was charged with federal obstruction of justice. The grand jury indictment alleged that he tampered with evidence by driving Jason's BMW from the storage locker in Nevada to California on December 26, 2004, and that he washed the interior and exterior of the car, abetting Jason in the November 29, 2004 slaying of an armored guard at an Ahwatukee Foothills theater. For his $600,000 bail, his wife, in-laws, and my mom put up their houses as collateral.

I drove Brad to court hearings in Arizona, got hotel rooms, and helped him sort through some of his bills. When the next-door neighbor took spray paint and wrote "killer murderer" all over his garage, I banged on the guy's door and let him have it. I told him my brother Brad was not the murderer and he had children. I scared the crap out of him. I'd basically had it with people judging us.

Brad eventually plea bargained to a lesser count of providing false information. He was given three years supervised probation. The FBI agents on the case were not happy with the verdict because they truly thought he'd be in jail for years awaiting trial, but the ordeal ruined his life. He owed his attorney nearly $500,000 and he wasn't going to be able to get his contractor's license because he was now a felon and was on the verge of losing his house.

I continued to do my best to help him however I could. We had never been close, but now with Jason gone, we only had each other and this trauma had actually bonded us in a weird way.

At least I thought it had.

One day, after I had given his younger daughter some clothes, Brad called and accused me of badmouthing him to her.

"I did not," I said.

"I'll never speak to you again if you badmouth my kids in front of me," he said as though I hadn't just denied it.

I understood he was in a bad place and wanted to talk things out with him, so I went over to see him. He was in the backyard and Jason's stuff was everywhere—dirt bikes, wave runners, all of Jason's toys from the storage unit in Las Vegas. "Brad, can we please talk? I want to discuss what it is you think I said."

"You need to get out of here right now. I'm going to call the sheriff on you. You're on private property."

"I'm your sister. I just helped you get through this whole ordeal. What are you talking about?"

"You need to get out of here right now," he said not even making eye contact. He was cold and emotionless.

"How can you do this?" I was already crying, but I began balling my head off. "I don't want to lose another brother."

"Get out of here or I'm going to call the sheriff," he said. "I never want to speak to you or see you again for the rest of my life."

My last truly happy memories of Brad were from long before Jason's or my dad's disappearances. I remember walking up and down the hospital hallway with him while I was in labor with Logan. I have great memories of spending time together in Houston a few years later for my son's birthday, and more memories watching and caring for his three children, going to the beach, and spending holidays together.

Now, I had yet another brother I would never see again.

# LOST CONNECTIONS

Right after Jason's disappearance, I was so distraught, I couldn't eat or sleep. I hid in the house, leaving only to get Logan to and from school.

As a designer, it is my job to know my clients. Before I go into business with somebody for four or five years, I have to get a read on them. In the first hour I meet someone, I'm always thinking, is this something I want to deal with? I thought I knew my brother and what he was and wasn't capable of. The idea that I saw nothing different in the week I spent with him haunted me day and night.

I began to search the internet for anything I could find about my brother and the incident. There were multiple theories based on the varying reports. One eyewitness said the shooter was Hispanic. Did that mean Jason was falsely identified? A different witness reported they'd seen Jason talking to another man in the foyer of the theater—as in a potential accomplice who'd actually committed the crime and not my brother? Since Jason was apparently casing out the area, eating at nearby restaurants for a nearly a week, was it possible that he was just the getaway driver?

I simply found it impossible to believe that my brother, who'd never done anything violent in the past, could have committed such a sudden, brutal, cold-blooded, pre-meditated murder.

The bicycle found nearby had Jason's prints on it, but what if his accomplice, the actual killer, rode Jason's bike away from the scene wearing gloves while Jason drove to a pre-arranged meet-up location? Maybe the accomplice somehow secretly ditched the bike while they were speeding away in order to get his part of the cash and frame Jason for the actual killing? The police admitted that without that piece of evidence they wouldn't have had a lead at all, much less a suspect. The Jason I knew was smart and meticulous. He would never abandon a bicycle used to flee the scene of a crime, and definitely not one with his fingerprints on it.

If Jason actually did commit this crime, then why was he back at my house acting so "normal," and out in the public eye? Perhaps he was involved, but did not actually carry out the shooting? If he did, then why did he just not take off and disappear at the time? Why come to me and wait it out?

Given he was depressed for the last year before the crime and hanging out by himself, he'd probably been chased by creditors, had no real job, and felt increasingly desperate.

Desperate enough to kill someone to get his life back on track?

Did he think he was going to get away with what he done? Was it because he didn't know the bike had his fingerprints on it? He had to know they would find the bike. He was smart enough to evade the FBI for sixteen years, but not smart enough to wipe the bike down?

My mind just kept going back to what was his thinking, if he *was* thinking, and how, despite everything we'd been through as kids and adults, Jason could murder someone in cold blood for any amount of money. The thought of my brother shooting someone at point blank range was endlessly haunting.

Logan caught mononucleosis soon after Jason's exit and I got it as well. The Jason situation had taken a devastating toll on both of us. The combination of stress and sickness wiped out our immune systems to such a huge extent that we both still suffer from chronic fatigue. Logan recovered but got behind in school and began to lose his drive for basketball. He hated wearing a Catholic school uniform and going to religious classes. He complained that he'd only agreed to go in the first place to please James.

It took three months before I was able to force myself to get up and go back out into the world. Finally, I made an appointment with a personal trainer and paid in advance so I would actually go. I knew working out would help more than anything else.

I met a guy at the gym. Coincidentally, we'd met once before when I was out with Jason the week he was visiting.

"I met you and your brother," he said.

"My brother's long gone," I said.

"What happened?" he asked.

I felt like I'd been abandoned by my mother when she'd moved to Alaska. My first husband had died. My father and brother had disappeared, and now my older brother never wanted to speak to or see me again. My whole life was abandonment. I had developed two methods of survival—one was to get close to somebody good like James, but then cause a problem and get out before they hurt me. The second was to find someone I could trust to be entirely undependable.

This guy was the latter—a narcissist, sociopath, sex and exercise addict, who did steroids and lots of cocaine. In other words, perfect for me. He had two Porsches, an SUV and a convertible. I was drawn to him because he reminded me of Jason and all the things Jason and I liked to do together—party, play sports, and compete with each other. Not the typical father figure type I was normally attracted to, because he was close to my age, but equally destructive. A competitive triathlete, he'd take me to the gym in the morning and on fifteen mile mountain bike or fifty mile road bike rides in the afternoon. He kept a strict six day per week training schedule: train at 4:30 AM, again around 2:00 PM, dinner at 4:30 PM and sleep by 8:00 PM. Honestly, I liked the discipline. I liked having a schedule because it kept my mind occupied. I'd nap while he was at work midday so I had the energy to go on a bike ride with him in the afternoon. I didn't want him to think I was too weak for his regimented training schedules.

The working out was compulsive, like him, but I could deal with it. In fact, I was so exhausted I couldn't think. What I couldn't stomach was that I found out he was married three months into the relationship. His wife tried to throw a paver through his living room window. I ran out to see what was going on by the pool, and she was clearly drunk and distraught. I brought her inside and tried to reassure her I had no idea he was married. When he appeared to see what was going on, things got physical between them and I found myself trying to help her. She cut herself with a broken wine glass and blood was everywhere.

Even worse, I wasn't the only other woman in his life. He was just like the other men who would pick a fight on a Thursday or Friday so they had the weekend for their other conquests. Narcissists are like vampires—they need a constant new blood supply. If one woman is not meeting their needs or they are bored, they find another chick to get their fix.

Thank goodness Logan wanted to spend his senior year back in Laguna with his friends so I had a way out. Besides, this narcissist liked his conquests spread out geographically so he wouldn't get caught. As soon as Logan's school year in Rancho Santa Margarita ended, I got away from my bad choice by moving back to Laguna Beach, ignoring all the *I love you, only you* calls and the gifts (he loved to give me sporting equipment). He wanted back what he could no longer have.

But again, it was not about me, it was all about him and the chase.

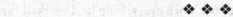

Logan started his senior year of high school back in Laguna. James moved when we did and bought a place down the street. I hated the ever-present whispers about my brother, but Laguna was home, so I leaned into it and further established my presence by renting a storefront office.

My father and brothers had no work ethic at all. My mother taught school until I was born, and then dedicated her life to being a mom. She once said to me, "I'm not like you, Jami. You go out and make things happen. You're a people person It takes a special kind of person to do what you do."

It was a huge compliment I didn't take lightly. In truth though, work was a lifeline and the only way to distract myself from thinking too much.

Logan tried to distract himself by playing basketball with his old teammates. He was beginning to show glimmers of his old self again when he was jumped on the court during the Martin Luther King basketball tournament in Long Beach. The opposing team coach wanted to win, so he told his players to take down the shooter scoring all the points. When Logan went in for a three-pointer, some kids jumped him and broke his arm in three places. It was recruiting season. Logan, who had all the best college recruiters scouting him at the game, didn't get a single offer.

For years, James had him taking free throw shots a hundred times a day. Logan had broken every Laguna Beach High School record in basketball and averaged thirty-three points a game. In his mind, he was a superstar 6'1" leftie with such a high vertical, he could jump over the top of guys who were 6' 6". With everything he'd worked for since he was five gone—not to mention his dad, his grandfather, and his uncle, best friend, and idol Jason—Logan lost interest in almost everything.

In his mind, his "game" was over.

In the midst of doing everything I could to glue my son back together, I was getting calls from various law enforcement entities. The Orange County Sheriff's Missing Person's department had been in contact since my father disappeared in 1994. The message they left was almost always the same: "This is Orange County Sheriff's Department, Missing Persons. We want to talk to you about your dad, David John Brown. Can you please give us a call?"

My heart would beat a little faster as I called back hopeful that I was finally going to learn for certain what became of my dad, one way or another. Instead, it always the same story: "Have you heard anything?"

"No I haven't heard anything!" I said, irritated and disappointed. "Why do you leave messages like that on my phone?"

They never had a good answer.

Now, and in addition, I had the FBI calling and stopping by my house, sometimes twice a week. Their questions were always the same as well: *Have you heard from Jason? We need some more information. Could you tell us this story again? You need to tell us when you move. You need to tell us what's going on. You need to keep us in the loop. Have you heard anything?*

I would always answer the same way: *I don't know anything.*

I spent night after night awake and agonizing about my son, the FBI, and our future. To this day, I have a major insomnia. I have had to train myself to go to bed through guided sleep hypnosis meditations. I think it's part of my post-traumatic stress disorder. It could even be pre-traumatic stress disorder, thinking tonight is the night my phone is going to ring and I'm going to hear that they found Jason or my Dad dead—or worse—alive.

Every time I heard a noise at the door or a car idling outside I thought, *who's going to save us?*

The answer was, of course, no one but me.

# INDIA

Thankfully, Logan's arm recovered. He was not eligible for a Division One scholarship and would have to walk on for a year to "get back on the map." Instead, he took a scholarship to Utah Valley, one of the top Division Two universities for basketball. A year later, one of the coaches from Utah Valley transferred to another Division Two school in Twin Falls, Idaho where a lot of kids who got in trouble for grades and other problems went for a year in order to get back to a D1 school. This coach loved Logan and offered him a free ride. Life was headed in a positive direction when, one morning, I got a call from the coach.

"I'm looking for Logan."

"He's not here. He's there, at school," I said, wondering what the hell was going on.

"He's not here. He's missing."

"What do you mean…?" I couldn't even utter the word missing. It made me physically ill. "You're the one who's supposed to have him."

"He took off."

"Took off where?"

"That's what I'm trying to figure out."

I left frantic messages every place I could think of. Finally, James called. "Logan is here with me. He showed up in the middle of the night."

"Thank God," I said, overwhelmed with relief.

"The thing is, he says he's not going back."

"Meaning he wants to transfer?"

"He says he's not going back to school at all."

"He needs to get his ass back there," I said, my relief turning into instant irritation. "He's been through so much to get to this point."

"Believe me, I agree, but I've been up all night talking to him and his mind's made up," James said.

"My turn," I said.

"Good luck."

"You scared the shit out of me, Logan," I said, waking him at James's house.

"I'm sorry, Mom, but I wasn't missing," Logan said. "I came home."

My son had always been a numbers wizard and I had dreams of him being a famous sports commentator with ESPN. Home wasn't where he was supposed to be. "You belong in school."

"That's just it. I don't."

"What about basketball?"

"Basketball is James's dream, not mine. I wanted to make him proud, but I hate that place and I hate being in school. It's not where I belong right now. I hate Utah. I don't belong in school."

"Where do you belong then?"

"I want to go travel. I want to go live in India."

"India?" I asked, wondering how it was my spoiled little kid from Orange County had come up with going to such a place, and how he'd ever manage there.

"I need to go find myself," he said.

It quickly became clear that my little boy, who I loved to dress up as a child, and do his hair, who claimed he was hugged and loved too much as a kid, had made up his mind and I wasn't going to be able to say or do anything to change what he'd decided to do.

Logan walked out of his basketball scholarship and went to India and then Thailand, where he lived in a hut with no running water or electricity.

He came back more spiritual and entirely unconcerned with materialistic things.

I was relieved, but slightly leery about how long his newfound Zen would last. After all, he carried around far too many Brown genes.

# AFTERSHOCKS

One of Jason's so-called acquaintances pulled up to a stop light near the Salt Lake City Hogle Zoo and said he saw Jason, tan, with longer hair, behind the wheel of a car. He turned, looked, ran the red light, and disappeared. On another occasion, the police apprehended Sean Penn's body double because Jason is a dead ringer for the actor. There were supposed sightings in places as far flung as Bali, Indonesia, Idaho, and a wilderness glimpse of someone who fit the description of my brother in Iron County in southwest Utah.

Even though Jason continued to evade capture, the FBI remained confident he would be apprehended, so much so that on December 8, 2007, exactly 1,104 days after the murder, Jason became the 489th person to be placed on the United States Federal Bureau of Investigation's Ten Most Wanted Fugitives list.

I compartmentalized and tucked away the intense pain of what had happened and what could still be ahead by putting everything into JD Martin Design. Big clients continued to roll in. I hired an assistant, bought a sports car for personal use, an SUV for work, and started dating an architect. He was a nice man, but had no money to speak of, which suited me just fine. I didn't need a man to support me. Besides, I wanted to try something different for once instead of the usual obsessive-compulsive womanizing narcissist. I wanted someone I could boss around and trust which, in my mind, equaled no problems. We traveled in Switzerland, snowboarding for a month. We went to Moab on mountain biking trips and other adventures. The relationship provided a pleasant, if not permanent, diversion.

I continued to get word of mouth referrals. People would see my work and new projects materialized. I'd gut houses and rebuild them, running up to 120 subs like a general contractor. I would pull owner/builder permits and get to work. I designed multiple prime ocean front properties. I spent one year doing a total renovation of a yacht in San Diego—tearing the whole thing apart and revamping it complete with a Jacuzzi on top.

All I really cared about was work and not dealing with thoughts of Jason.

I got in a car accident in my sports car and injured my neck badly. I was messed up physically, and on pain medication, but I kept working. I took on multiple jobs at once because action was the distraction.

Except for when it wasn't.

In high school, Logan, who is a math and sports stats genius, would stay up all night playing party poker, winning tens of thousands of dollars. He was also a sports addict. While most kids watched cartoons, Logan had been watching ESPN since he was two. He knew every stat of every sports score of every game. He came back from India changed, but the family penchant for gambling was alive and well in my son. Logan found his way into high-roller status at the Bellagio and moved the sports betting line to the point where they put him up for almost three months.

At the end of his stint at the Bellagio, Logan moved to Florida with a buddy. While he was away from Las Vegas, he quickly found his way to the Indian casinos and got right back into poker and assorted other gambling. Inevitably, Logan got involved with bookies and ended up owing them money. They came looking for him and roughed up his roommate who they forced to give my contact information. Not only did I find myself reliving all of the crap from my dad and Jason all over again, but I had to go into hiding when Logan, who was already in hiding himself, warned me to get out of my house. The bookies were going to kill me if he didn't come up with the money he owed them ASAP.

James paid them off.

In the aftermath, Logan promised us he wouldn't gamble anymore. As he was driving back home though, he hooked up with a woman who became pregnant. A year later, we found out he had a baby daughter. Upon learning the news he was a dad, Logan moved to Texas to help raise his little girl.

No matter what else was happening in my life, the FBI agents were in constant contact. At first, I would get calls insisting, "We need to meet right now."

"I can't," I'd say. "I'm working."

"It doesn't matter what you're doing. You need to meet us," whoever it was would say, or they'd just knock on my door and expect me to let them right in.

In the first years after Jason went missing, agents would show up in my neighborhood, knock on my neighbor's doors, and say, "Hi, we need some information on Jami because her brother is on the FBI's Most Wanted list. Can we come in and talk to you?"

It was so embarrassing to have to face them later, walking the streets of Laguna. They all knew. When I moved from North Laguna to South Laguna, the FBI canvased the whole neighborhood telling everyone, "We're looking for Jami Martin."

All they had to do was Google my business address and phone number. I was so embarrassed, I called the Los Angeles office and asked, "Why are you going around my neighborhood and humiliating me and ruining my reputation?"

"We didn't know where you moved."

"I run a business in Laguna! My business address and phone number are listed everywhere. Google me. I am an open book. My phone number and my website are right there, even my work address." I dared to say to the investigator. "How the hell are you ever going to find my brother when I moved five miles away and you couldn't find me? How lame are you guys?"

Over time, the visits slowed down from weekly, to monthly, and then, eventually, I only got a call about every other month. Whenever a new investigator came on board, he or she was inevitably convinced they were going to solve the case and I had to deal with a predictable scenario that played out like this:

"I need to re-interview you because we lost the tapes," or "We lost important evidence."

"You lost the evidence in a murder investigation?" I'd ask.

"Yeah, it's missing. We have to start all over."

"I have nothing new to say," I'd tell them.

"Well, we need to hear it again."

I met them wherever they wanted to meet. I told them whatever they wanted to hear. Wherever they wanted me to be, whatever pictures they wanted me to look at, whatever they wanted to talk about, I did as I was told. I fully cooperated, because I knew they could take me to jail for obstruction of justice at any time. They made me nervous by turning the recorder on and off and telling me certain stuff was off the record, but I knew it wouldn't be. Even though no one ever came out and said it, they clearly enjoyed the power of holding the threat of jail over my head.

Interspersed with the routine check-ins, I would get the occasional calls to identify photos and even bodies at the morgue. If they couldn't identify someone, or if they found a body in Oregon out in the middle of nowhere, they would contact me and say, "We found your brother."

"Okay," I'd say, anxious, doubtful, and stressed.

If I was lucky, and it was just a photo, I could look at the clothes and know it wasn't him. "He wouldn't wear that and this person's feet are huge. It's not my brother."

I was called in once to identify a man they'd found in an Oregon ditch who had, "Really bad teeth—a meth addict."

"Jason didn't do meth," I said.

"Does he have dental records?"

"Not that I know of," I said. "He rarely went to the dentist because his teeth were perfect. My dad had the same perfect teeth."

Needless to say, it wasn't him.

# So Tired

In 2010, I was at an afternoon birthday celebration at a restaurant on the beach. It was a long hot day, and it was getting dark. My new Porsche was parked in a nearby lot. Because I was planning to stay a bit longer and jump a cab home, I decided to move my car to a spot where I could leave it overnight. I'd gotten a DUI a few years earlier driving home from dinner at Morton's Steakhouse. I'd only had a couple of drinks with food that evening so I didn't hesitate to take the breathalyzer. I blew a .08 and the officer had no choice but take me in. I definitely didn't want to go through that experience again, so I needed to move the car.

The valet parking attendant directed me across the highway to a nearby lot that had a 24-hour policy.

As soon as I moved my vehicle, a motorcycle cop came flying up to me.

"What kind of car is that?" he asked.

"It's the new Porsche Cayman," I said.

"Yours?"

I nodded and started walking back toward the restaurant.

"Why isn't there a license plate on it?" he asked following me.

"Because it's brand new." I was a little flippant, but I was also anxious to get back to my friends and wasn't into dealing with a flirtatious cop with nothing better to do than pester me.

"Have you been drinking?" he asked.

"A little," I said pointing to the restaurant. "I'm over there with my friends at a birthday party."

"Did you just move your car?"

"I was parking it in an overnight lot because I'm planning to get a cab home later. I wasn't driving down the road drunk."

"But you did drive it?"

"Yes," I said. "You're not really going to do this to me for moving my car so I can leave it overnight and not drive drunk?"

He called for backup and the next thing I knew, they were trying to give me a breathalyzer.

This time, I refused.

The cop put me in his car but decided to have mercy on me by "letting me" sit up front instead of in back like a garden variety criminal. I got in the front seat and he handcuffed me. Needless to say, I wasn't a superfan of law enforcement in general, or that guy in particular. Plus, I was completely pissed off that he'd decided to give me trouble because I was a blonde with a Porsche. He had a Big Gulp in the cup holder, so when he entered the sheriff's department lot, I leaned over and *big gulped* his entire soda.

"You did not just drink that whole thing," he said.

I shrugged.

"I'm going to be in so much trouble."

"That makes two of us," I said.

"You can't tell anyone you drank that," he said.

I shrugged again and delayed doing the breathalyzer a second time. When I finally agreed, I received my second DUI.

I was not given jail time, but I was put on house arrest for forty-five days and forced to wear an ankle monitor. I could only go to AA meetings and walk to work. I had to pay insurance and payments on the two cars I owned but couldn't drive either of them for a year. I couldn't technically leave my house so I'd lay out on the deck with my foot inside the door. At the time, I was living with the architect, but I needed to suffer alone, so I ended the relationship and sent him on his way.

True to form, I went to my AA meetings, managed to take care of my clients, and did everything I was supposed to do. I did not allow myself to think about how hard it all was, I just barreled through it all wearing my clunky, embarrassing ankle bracelet, not realizing I was absolutely suffocating beneath the ever-growing layers of grief, pain, and stress.

I began seeing a wealthy guy who was just a few years older than me. Predictably, he was alcoholic and showered me with gifts. I was definitely self-medicating with alcohol, and taking a lot of sleeping pills, as well as pain pills for the neck injury that never completely went away. Then, I tore both Achilles's tendons. I had to have two separate surgeries, allowing one foot to heal before I could do the other, and resulting in a full year where I couldn't walk or run or play tennis. Instead of working out, I cried.

I searched hard for the lesson to be learned and came to the conclusion that the universe wanted me to STOP. Stop and breathe. I was not able to run around to distract myself from dealing with the overwhelming pain. I had to be alone with myself and somehow get through all of this emotional baggage I was carrying around.

I was so tired of being strong. I just couldn't do it anymore. It was too hard to get up in the morning, especially after endless nights filled with insomnia. I just couldn't face all the shit I'd been facing. I'd lost my dad and my brother and my son's father. My remaining brother no longer spoke to me. Everything but my career was a mess. The only time I didn't feel pain was when I was asleep and I could barely get to sleep, much less stay that way.

Even though I lived in Laguna, I liked to check into the famed oceanfront Montage Resort to escape from everything and everybody, hang out by the pool, and go to the spa. I made a reservation and made plans to meet Antonio for dinner. I'd already been back and forth with him for years when Jason disappeared and we'd remained friends. He'd become my caretaker—the rescuer, a safety net, and someone I could trust.

When I said goodbye to Antonio for the evening, my plan was to go upstairs, take a bunch of Ambien, and throw the bottle on top of the building so it looked like I drank some alcohol so it interacted with the sleeping pills. I wanted it to look like I'd overdosed, not that I killed myself—for Logan's sake. In my head, I did not really want to die, I just wanted to go to sleep for a long time. I was exhausted from life. I was exhausted from living. They would find me in the morning—asleep forever.

I ran a bubble bath, then put on a silky nightgown. I was already pretty lit when I put the DO NOT DISTURB sign on the door, took the handful of Ambien, and threw the bottle onto the roof as planned. I remember trying to walk to the bed but not making it all the way. I wanted to stop swimming against the tormented tide of emotional trauma and let it slowly carry me out...

I woke up in ICU with black charcoal on my face and wearing an oxygen mask.

My first thought was, "Shit. I woke up."

Logan and James were looking down at me.

"Why did you do this, Mom?" Logan asked with tears streaming down his face.

I was mad I'd woken up, ashamed that I'd actually gone through with it, and sad I had to face the aftermath and the stigma of not succeeding. But as I looked at my son's anguished face, it sobered me up to what I had done. I hadn't thought about those who loved me that I would leave behind.

"I'm so sorry," was all I could say.

"Don't ever do that again, Mom," Logan said.

I took way too many pills to have woken up but, somehow, housekeeping found me in time. I have no memory of being found, or the ambulance, or being revived, but I was alive. It was a defining moment in my life. I realized I had more to accomplish on this earth. The Universe still had plans for me. It was almost like this event had to happen for me to appreciate the good in my life and how to move forward. It was time to change and stop self-sabotaging. I realized my survival had been a blessing. My son needed me as much as I needed him. I needed to stay in the fight, no matter what. If not for my sake, for Logan, who had suffered all the same losses.

# RECOVERY

When a person overdoses, they are typically put on a 5150 hold for seventy-two hours. The head physician at the hospital had kids Logan's age and knew me so I was able to convince the medical staff that my overdose was an accident borne out of trying to get a good night's sleep and not a suicide attempt, just like I'd planned. They never found the bottle of Ambien that I'd tossed on the roof, so my story was believable.

I managed to talk my way out of staying for the three full days, but I knew I needed help. I contacted my therapist, who happened to be named Dr. Ruth. Even though I hadn't met with her for a while, she knew my history and understood the pain I'd experienced losing my father and brother, as well as my relationship issues. She was about to retire, but she agreed to see me.

Together, we decided the best way for me to deal with the feelings of rage and abandonment that led me to try and take my life was to attend a program at a treatment center for addiction and psychological trauma called The Meadows in Wickenburg, Arizona. The program, called Survivor's Workshop, consisted of two weeks of super-intense behavioral emotive therapy geared to help trauma patients deal with serious issues in a concentrated way.

Before attending, the patient must fill out detailed paperwork which is reviewed over a number of months until an ideal eight to ten-person group is assembled. Each of the people in a given group have parallels and are placed together to trigger issues and emotions that need to be addressed. When the group enters the program, they spend day and night together for two weeks. In my group, there was a fellow Mormon as well as people who reminded me of my mother, father, and brother. As part of the therapy, a patient acts out the trauma they've experienced doing visualizations where the people who trigger you are brought into the scenario. In other words, I spent two weeks with "Jason" and "Dad" and "Mom" sitting across from me.

In a typical session, the therapist darkened the room. When it was my turn, I was put into a trancelike state until I believed the people I needed to deal with were there.

"Jami is going to say everything she feels," the therapist said to the woman who resembled my mother. "You're going to listen to Jami and hear what she has to tell you."

In this setting, with my fellow patients observing, I let "Mom" have it, getting everything out I felt toward her but couldn't say to her face: "Why did you stay married to a monster and keep having more children? How could you do that to me? How could you divorce Dad and leave us during this important time in our lives? It's your fault Jason did what he did because if you hadn't left us, it would have never happened!"

I sobbed and told "Mom" off and then the therapist "kicked" her out of the room.

When "Dad" came in, I shouted, "You're such a liar. You're such a crook. I loved you so much. Why would you just leave me all alone?

I needed you. I know it's good you are gone but you're still my dad. Where did you go? Why?"

"Why did you do this?" I screamed over and over at "Jason." "How could you do this? Why did you lie to me? How could you betray me? You were my brother and my best friend!"

After the session, patients release the anger they've been holding inside by throwing, screaming at, or beating something. It's a method of moving all of the pain out of the body and soul, and no longer stuffing these intense feelings. When you stuff, you medicate through food, alcohol, and relationships, never dealing with the intense pain at your core. Some patients screamed it out. Others threw tissue boxes against the wall. I chose the most aggressive option which was to beat a bat against a big foam pad.

Needless to say, I beat that thing until I literally passed out from exhaustion and was on the ground, hands red and crying. In other words, everyone in the group had their chance to confront their situations, pull all the emotions out, and then release them with a physical action.

I heard horrible things in my group and felt lucky I was never raped or suffered through some of the experiences I helped others exorcise. And yet, it came as a shock to me that most everyone considered my story the toughest of all.

I'd experienced so much loss it almost seemed normal.

When I got home, I called my mom and asked, "Why didn't you wait until we graduated from high school to divorce Dad? So much would never have never happened if you hadn't have left us with a monster. Why did you leave?"

"Why are you doing this to me, Jami?" she answered.

"I'm not doing anything to you," I said. "I understand that he was a con artist and a criminal, and that it was really hard, but what was wrong with staying a few more years until we were old enough to get by without you?"

There was silence on the other end of the line. Finally, she said, "I couldn't take it anymore."

It helped to hear her say it. I had finally begun to understand why she left. I saw that she had no other choice to keep her sanity, no matter the outcome. I think she truly thought she would keep us kids and the house, but it did not play out that way.

As a result of doing the hard work of dealing with all the pain I had been stuffing down, I stopped crying every time I talked about Jason, Dad, and even Brad.

My aunt once asked, do you want to have a funeral for them?

"Why would I have a funeral for them? They're not dead."

From going through this intense therapy, I came to terms with the fact that no matter what did or didn't become of Dad and Jason, I was alive and needed to live my life.

The Meadows woke me up to myself but there was still much work to be done. I wrote letters that I never sent, saw a therapist on my own, and did Bikram yoga five days a week. I was told before The Meadows by numerous therapists that I would need ten years of therapy to get through this stuff. In my mind, I didn't have time or the desire for ten years of counseling and became determined to do what needed to be done myself. I knew my role in life was not to play victim or wallow in all the craziness I'd lived through, but to rise above and beyond somehow. Before, I figured if I looked put together, my clothes, my home, my car, then no one would know how broken I was on the inside. It was time to change that. I have always been intrigued by psychology and more specifically self-help and spiritual thought, so I dove in. I bought and read every author and book I could get my hands on: Tony Robbins, Marianne Williamson, Eckhart Tolle, Deepak Chopra, Wayne Dyer, Thich Nhat Hanh, the Dalai Lama, and more.

I also went to our Mormon church and told them everything—as in everything I'd ever done. Much like going to a priest and confessing your sins, it felt really good to purge and get it all out. They did not excommunicate me, instead, they disfellowshipped me for a time, then reinstated me. I think the bishop knew that after all I had endured, I would fall out of the church for good if they took more drastic action. The church was probably the one constant in my life. Without it in my earlier years, I would have fallen into the same ways of John Brown. It taught me a value system. It taught me right from wrong.

As part of my reinstatement, I had to go to church for a year, be active and attend meetings, follow the word of wisdom, and take a calling. Even though I didn't buy a lot of what I was being sold, I gave it my all. As my calling, I had all the primary kids draw their favorite scripture and use their drawings as the cover for the weekly programs. The kids loved seeing the art on the cover and I loved being involved. I also did my best to continue progressing.

During this time, one of the more memorably aggressive FBI agents turned up to question me— an attractive female agent named Anastasia who was determined to solve the case.

"We need to meet," she said, calling out of nowhere.

"Okay," I said, like I always did. "I'll meet you at the coffee shop in Boat Canyon in North Laguna."

I showed up a little late and spotted her sitting at an outside table with another agent.

As I walked by them to go get my coffee, she said. "Do you think there's time to be wasted here?"

"I'm sorry I'm late," I said. "I had some work I had to wrap up first."

"This can end really good for you or really bad," she said. "It's your decision."

As I sat down for yet another rehashing of all the information I'd repeatedly given the FBI, Anastasia continued to get more and more ramped up, her voice growing louder and more aggressive.

After a while, I was just over it. "I've got things to do," I said, looking at my watch and noting that it was already past 10:00 AM. "I've got to go to work."

As I was getting up, four Laguna Beach police cars came racing up and surrounded the café. The officers got out of their vehicles, used their doors for shields, and shouted, "Laguna Beach Police Department, get your hands up!"

Anastasia got up, opened her jacket and announced, "FBI!"

There was a second of confusion before everyone re-holstered the many guns pointed in our direction.

"What's the problem?" Anastasia asked. "Why is this happening?"

"Somebody called in saying there was a heated conversation, and that one of the ladies sitting at the tables outside had a gun in her jacket."

"You've got to be kidding me," I said. "This is so mortifying."

And it was. I knew everyone in town and now they were getting dragged into the insanity. People I went to high school with were there witnessing the incident.

"I'm so sorry about this," I said to the guy behind the counter as soon as the fuss died down.

"It's okay," he said kindly, "I have a family member hiding out in another country, too."

At that moment, I knew I needed to get out of Laguna Beach. I couldn't go to the post office without hearing people whisper, "That's Jason's sister," or come up to me and ask, "Have they found your brother?" Everyone knew me and what had happened in my family and I'd had enough of the public humiliation. I didn't feel comfortable unless I was moving, and I hadn't stayed in any one place for very long since I'd left Laguna for college. I had business coming in from all over the country and I didn't need to be in Laguna Beach or anywhere near to be successful.

It was time for a fresh start somewhere entirely new.

# ACTION IS THE DISTRACTION

I had just returned recently from a two month design project in Park City, Utah. As I drove back into Laguna after twelve hours on the road, I thought, *the mountains. I need to heal in the mountains away from anyone that knows my name or my family*. A new beginning.

I'd fallen in love with the wide open spaces, the large trees, the four seasons, the new adventures in the snow with all the winter activities. I could learn to fly fish in the summer (which I did and became quite good) and ride my mountain bike all over those endless mountain ranges. It was like Laguna Beach in the mountains, except no one knew Jami Brown.

I moved to Park City in 2013. Of course, Antonio appeared a few week later, saying he was meeting some investors about a potential ski resort. Thankfully, the deal fell through. The distance served us well. I had pulled off his mask and he soon found another energy source upon which to feed.

I settled in, and quickly met Tony. He was Italian and a retired banker from the East Coast who seemed very honest and put together. He also definitely fit my profile—older, a father figure, generous, etc., etc., We had an amazing time traveling together. His hobbies included racehorses, and of course betting on racehorses, as well as lots of skiing and fishing. Because he was retired, he had plenty of time for me. He had an amazing circle of "normal" friends, which I liked. He taught me how to be a fly fisherwoman, and, after multiple concussions in the snowboard park, got me off my snowboard and on to a pair of skis. We were a good team. His love for his racehorses included many trips to Kentucky and to the infamous Kentucky Derby. He was kind and thoughtful, but there was one rule: he would only buy me gifts that were related to sports, although he did buy me a string of pearls, once. He was controlling to be sure, but weren't all the men I chose? It's like they all thought they were going to be the one guy who could tame the wild stallion, Jami.

While we were seeing each other, he contracted H1N1. I got really sick as well, but Tony endured a medical odyssey in which he was put into a medically induced coma, intubated, contracted sepsis, died twice, had a stroke which left him temporarily paralyzed and was brought back to life.

I let his ex-wife into his house during that time so she and their daughter could be there for him. At the time, Tony's ex was in the middle of a divorce from the man she'd married after him and had nowhere to go. People get crazy when someone is on their deathbed, and his family wanted me out of the picture completely. It didn't hurt that there was money involved. Out of nowhere, I wasn't allowed to visit him in the hospital and I wasn't welcome in his house. Unwilling to fight what seemed to be a losing battle, I took off.

When Tony awoke from the coma he asked, "Where's Jami?"

"Jami left you," he was told, and, thinking I'd abandoned him in his time of need, he and his ex got back together.

I began seeing Eric, a handsome, fit man, who was my age and was, like me, an inactive Mormon. This time, I went for a Jason twin— athletic, muscular, addicted to golf and, of course, a charmer. I liked that Eric sold cars for a living and didn't have much money, which I took as a positive because, once again, I thought I could control everything and be in charge. I would support us. I would wear the pants. It was the formula for success that had eluded me. I told my- self he reminded me of Jason in all the good ways—we golfed and mountain-biked constantly.

We got engaged quickly and I paid for our wedding in Las Vegas at the top of the Trump hotel, surrounded by all my friends.

Everything was newlywed bliss for a week. Then, I found porn on his phone. Having been through too much with too many cheating, porn-obsessed men, but clearly not yet over my addiction to that kind of man, I freaked out.

Eric admitted to both me and his kids that he had a sex addiction. I had caught him lying, but he promised he would take any and all steps necessary to erase this issue from his life. I wasn't happy, but we were married and I could live with it, as long as he kept his word. I kept telling myself that everyone has something. I had chosen a life of men who mimicked my childhood and this behavior was totally par for the course. The problem, of course, was there was more. My average joe, who I assumed I could dress up and mold into some- thing successful was keeping a few more secrets: he gambled, smoked a lot of weed, and was a convicted felon with a hot head and temper. He almost beat a guy to death he found in bed with his ex girlfriend.

I knew I'd made a big mistake, but I soon had a bigger concern. I went to the doctor with some really dark patches on my chest. In

Laguna, and in college on Oahu, we used to rub our bodies with baby oil and lay on foil. I never used sunscreen and I lived for tennis and outdoor sports. In the past, every time I'd gone to the doctor with a mole or spot, they'd removed some of them and burned off others. This time, the doctor cut a big hole and dug out a mass of tissue. A biopsy revealed skin cancer. In total, I had over thirty melanomas on my chest, each of which had to either be dug out and cauterized.

The doctors were able to get all of the cancerous spots before they spread any further, but I had to have a round of both internal and external chemotherapy. I rubbed topical chemo cream on my skin which turned the cauterized scabs into excruciating open sores. As a result of the internal treatments, my hair thinned, I was throwing up constantly, and my memory became extremely fuzzy to the point where I struggled to put together sentences.

My career depended on keeping on top of all the jobs I had going and it was an extremely challenging time. I tried to keep my health issues quiet, but my clients, who were so used to my ability to juggle multiple details, began to notice I was struggling. Not only was I in awful pain, but I was throwing up in clients' bathrooms on the regular.

In my mind, I had to keep going because if I stopped, the whole world was going to crash in on me. I had just gotten married and I was the family breadwinner, but I was getting sicker and less able to work.

"You need to help me," I said to Eric, who, despite his other issues, was a hard worker.

I started sending him out to job sites to run project management for me. From my bed and sick from chemo, I started a company for him. I did the logos for the trucks. I came up with all the marketing. I set him up so he could work and I could rest until I felt better.

The business was and continues to be a success.

My relationship with Eric, however, was destined to go bust.

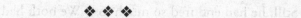

In the midst of regaining my health and on the verge of divorcing Eric, Logan who was now twenty-eight was finally starting to process some of the inevitable issues he'd been suppressing his entire life.

Logan called me one day and said he was struggling.

No one understood that feeling more than me, and it broke my heart.

There was no running away from our genetics and everything we'd been through. It inevitably bubbled to the surface and manifested itself. I knew it was time for him to deal with the pain because it was eating him alive, just like it had me.

"Come live with me," I told him. I put my divorce plans on hold and told myself I needed to act like everything was fine until I had Logan put back together. "Pack up your things, get in your car, and come to Park City right now."

Thankfully, Logan agreed. He arrived from Texas in as bad of shape as I expected. He'd been drinking and self-medicating in an all too familiar way and was on his way into a really dark hole.

We talked and talked for days.

He told me that I loved him and hugged him too much as a child, and that was why he does not like people hugging or touching him.

I thought to myself, Good. I accomplished that. I mean who can be loved too much?

I was definitely overprotective of my beautiful, golden child, and I never, ever disciplined him the way my father had me. I just poured endless amounts of love all over him.

Still, he had endured so much loss. We both had.

"You can you choose to be a victim of everything that's happened to us, or you can find a purpose," I told him. "I can say I'm this way because my dad did this to me and because I didn't have a mom growing up. You can act like that all day long, but in the end, you've got look at yourself in the mirror and you've got to get up in the morning. You need to have a purpose and your purpose can't be yourself—either a goal you want to achieve or your little girl who needs a dad. You didn't grow up with your dad, so you know what that's like."

I also put him to work for Eric. He'd never done any manual labor but learned a whole lot very quickly and was soon running crews.

When he was ready, I said, "You need to go home and be a dad and make your daughter your focus."

When he was back on his feet, he moved back to Texas. He got a job with a big landscaping company and loves what he does. Ironically, it's the same career that his dad chose. Logan is also a great father to his beautiful daughter.

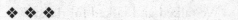

I tried my best to save my marriage with Eric, but it was doomed from the start. I had already put four years into our sham of a marriage, and I was miserable. The last two years were hell but I'd kept myself busy with traveling, work, and my friends.

I would catch Eric in lies, and he would look me straight in the eyes, and tell me another lie. He would twist things around and make them my fault. I would beg him to talk about his issues and he would run out the door to play golf without hesitation.

This was all too familiar. The breaking point for me was one day when his narcissist mask fell off. He was very depressed and begging me to help him. It was a trap. He didn't want help, he was bored. A narcissist needs constant stimulation. We were far gone from the "idealization phase," where he was on his best behavior—thoughtful, funny, kind, and super attentive, also known as love bombing. He was sitting at his desk with his hands over his head.

"I don't feel, Jami. I just don't feel anymore," he said.

I walked out of the office saying to myself, *Oh my GOD! He doesn't feel! I need to get away from him.*

It was a moment of clarity. I knew from past experience that getting away was not going to be easy, so I stood my ground despite his charm, gifts, and promises that he would change. I knew it was just a ploy to get me back.

Our relationship ended with him being led off in handcuffs in September 2018, as a result of his own actions

After all these years, I had broken the code. I would never allow myself to fall into the narcissist love trap again. I knew too much. I finally recognized how destructive my relationships with men who were identical to my father and brother truly were. I finally took a hard look at the similarities in the handsome, suave, successful men who drove me around in their flashy cars, plied me with gifts, and thought nothing of cheating on me. I knew my dad was crazy and that my brother stole things, but I started doing research into their pathology and the words *narcissist* and *sociopath* began to come up repeatedly.

I'd gone to The Meadows to deal with my abandonment issues, and now, years later, I was stuck and unhappy again. I had been divorced three times and had entered into yet another complicated situation. I realized it was time to recognize that the men I was most comfortable with were attracted to good looking, headstrong, independent women not because they appreciate them for who they are, or even the need to show them off, but to dominate and, in a sense, own them.

One night, awake as usual, I stumbled across an article in a yoga magazine about an ancient art in Ayurvedic medicine called "Panchakarma." In fact, the pages fell open on the table beside my bed as though I was supposed to read it. Developed for Indian royalty, I read that Panchakarma was a process, *to prolong life and health by removing physical impurities, bringing awareness to destructive thoughts and behaviors, and releasing old patterns.*

I had hit another rock bottom and I figured I had two choices—give up or get up and say enough is enough. It was time to stop racing down the same destructive path. I needed to find my way out, free myself and learn to recognize this pattern and avoid doing it again. I heeded the message and signed up for the ten day program at the Chopra Center in Carlsbad, California.

I decided to start the course right after New Year's. In order to do so, I was required to do a two week cleansing program ahead of my arrival, meaning there was no partaking in holiday festivities. That was fine because I was determined to follow through with my plan.

When my flight from Salt Lake City to San Diego was cancelled due to weather, I gladly paid double to get the last seat on a bigger plane.

I wasn't about to miss my first day.

While the Chopra center was as described, "a beautiful, nurturing place where people can come to heal their physical pain, find emotional freedom, empower themselves, and connect to their deepest spiritual self," Panchakarma is not for the weak. In fact it would prove to be one of the most demanding physical challenges I had ever attempted.

At the Chopra Center, no cell phones are permitted. You are unplugged to shut yourself off from the outside world and all of its distractions so you can connect and focus on your journey of healing. The days began and ended with meditation and yoga. I ate only kitchari in the morning and at lunch, while practicing what is called *mindful eating*, sometimes in silence. There were classes and instructors and a focus on the question, *who am I*, which we had to answer for ourselves daily. Days were filled with introspection and routine, both foreign concepts in my life.

The key facet of the program is known as the Five Actions or treatments. One of the treatments involved putting Ghee, which is clarified butter, in your eyes. As a result of the treatment, I found I could see more clearly when I spoke to people, like my inner vision wasn't cloudy anymore. Another was Shirodhara that involved slowly dripping oil on your third eye in the center of your head, which synchronizes brain waves and releases stress from the nervous system. With all the five treatments combined, it's like your inner world opens within and you discover more layers, deep buried emotions, and past traumas.

Unlike one of my century (100 mile bike races) which I could train for, my ten days at the Chopra Center were like being in a grueling spiritual race. Sometimes, it takes an experience this intense to wake up your spirit and shake you to your core. I had forgotten how, or maybe I had never known what it was like, to feed and care for my inner self. My sense of self had always been tied to other people and relationships. I was being pulled by everything just because I hurt so much inside.

At the end of my stay at the center, I decided to meet with one of their astrologers who also had a background as a physician, yogi, and poet. The astrologer informed me that I was in something known as a *chiron return* which only happens once every fifty years, or some say ages 49-52. I was about to turn 50 the following week. Astrology is very intricate and involved, but the gist of a chiron return is a turning point, where you completely transform your life and career, and experience profound healing.

Clearly, I was exactly where I needed to be.

# Girl—On The Go

My mom built me an amazing dollhouse when I was a child. I spent hours in a daydream re-arranging the furniture, making the beds, organizing the food in the kitchen, making it absolutely perfect. One of my interior design clients, a psychiatrist actually, said to me that he found it fascinating that I had made a successful career designing dollhouses for adults given I'd chosen a life where I moved around constantly.

My pattern had always been to make my home, design it perfectly (not to mention quickly), settle in, and then decide I needed a change. I have moved down the street, to a different city or, sometimes, to a different state altogether. I had to keep moving, meeting new people, doing new things, trying new things. *Action is the distraction* was always my motto and I came to accept that it was just my nature.

My friends refer to me as a high-end gypsy—a wanderer—putting down roots for an extended length of time has always made me feel anxious. I've always felt vulnerable when I get too comfortable because something will inevitably happen. Someone will lie, cheat, or leave me for sure, so I take off before any of that happens. While it's somewhat ironic, creating that special place for others has brought me sustained, undeniable joy.

I've always had a strong work ethic and tried my best to be honest in all my daily business dealings. I made sure my subs and workers were paid on time and kept my word, doing what I promised, as soon as money from my clients was in my hands. My integrity and my word were all I had. I'd learned from professionals like my dad and brother what not to do. I've always found myself in serving and helping people. Despite, or maybe because, of my past, my friends always called me when they were having issues. I was somehow the go-to person for all problems big and small. As a result, my clients trusted me that much more.

After working hand-in-hand with people for sometimes well over two years, and entrusted with the details of their day to day lives and often their bank accounts, I had numerous clients ask me to plan events, caretake their homes, organize their spaces, and manage the unmanageable aspects of their lives. Because I'd overseen numerous design and build projects across the country, and knew who to call, where to go, and what to do to get almost any job done, I started a time and lifestyle management company called Girl—on the Go.

Not only does Girl—on the Go deal with practical matters people need to conduct busy lives, but it has grown to include really helping people on another level. I've been able to take all the life experiences that have been thrown my way and help in the aftermath of a death, a cheating spouse, the body shame of not being pretty or thin enough, and much more.

Just as a contractor gathers up the contracts to finish the house, I gather up a team to help to gain control and help people live their best lives. I excel at helping to clean up messes—the messier the better. While I still design homes, I have found a secondary passion reorganizing and re-designing lives.

# Secrets, Lies, and the FBI

O ver the past decade and a half, Jason's crime has been featured on *Dateline*, *60 Minutes*, *American Greed*, and various other programs. Landing on the FBI's Most Wanted list and remaining there all these years captures people's attention. So does the $200,000 reward. *America's Most Wanted*, featuring John Walsh, ran the story on Jason for seven years before it went off the air in 2011. In that time, the FBI received more tips on Jason Derek Brown's case than any other fugitive portrayed on the show. I've been told it's because Jason has that average Southern California surfer boy next door look and is portrayed as rich, smart, and fun. None of the other fugitives on the FBI's top ten list have that appeal. Since the show's airing, twenty-three fugitives have been captured, one was killed, and three were found dead.

Jason has remained missing.

Chris Hanson from *Dateline* has called me numerous times over the past ten years trying to get me to do an interview. Every November, right around Thanksgiving when the crime happened, I get a call from *American Greed* or some other show wanting "my side" of the story. I always say no because I know that by the time the piece gets edited, produced, and then airs, my words will appear completely different than whatever it was I really said. In general, I avoid coverage about Jason and his crime because it is typically sensationalized and always filled with inaccuracies. The back and forth conjecture of the amateur detectives on the internet used to bother me even more. I haven't spoken much about Jason for all this time because I had to deal with the aftermath of being the sister of the all-American guy in the red hoodie beside Osama bin Laden on the Most Wanted poster. I'll never truly be able to get past the thought that he actually committed the cold-blooded act that landed him there.

I recently spoke to Adam, one of Jason's best friends, for the first time in sixteen years. It made me sad to look at Adam's social media photos and see him with his beautiful wife and children. I was sad because Jason can never have a life like that because of the choices he's made. I will never be able to share a family life like that with him.

"I think about Jason all the time. He was my best friend," Adam said, adding, "If I saw him again, the first thing I would do is hug him."

Adam related a story that happened before Jason arrived at my home, and before the alleged crime in Arizona. He said that Jason came to visit him and his new wife in Utah. They had a newborn baby and Jason came over with gifts and cooked them dinner. He told Adam that he was scared and was going to buy a gun for protection.

"That's crazy!" Adam said. "Why would you need a gun?"

Jason told Adam that he had gotten involved with a bad crowd in Las Vegas.

It sounded all too familiar.

When Jason left Adam's house, he said he would be back to snowboard with him in December.

After that visit, Jason bought the gun from Clark Aposhian in Utah. He went on to Arizona from there.

After the shooting, the FBI interviewed Adam. He remembered every detail, and recounted the question the question they asked all of us, "Where do you think he would go?"

Adam did not know either, but he did know one thing for sure, which he told them: "You are never going to find Jason Brown. He is the smartest person I know."

Periodically, Special Agent Lance Leising has flown out from Arizona to meet up with me in Laguna Beach or Park City so he can update me on new leads and information on the case. I hadn't spoken to him for a few years when I called to tell him I was writing this book.

I wanted his input and thoughts on my manuscript and, honestly, to make sure he wasn't going to arrest me for something I said or didn't tell him that he might read in the book.

"If I had wanted to throw you in prison, Jami, I would have done it a long time ago," he said.

Lance Leising has always been able to understand what I'm going through and empathize with me. Undoubtedly, it is because he has experience in situations like mine. He certainly witnessed first-hand the mental and emotional toll my brother's situation took on me during those first few years.

"How are you, Jami?" he has always asked at the beginning of every meeting. "How are things going for you?"

I appreciate that he wants to know about me first. If I haven't spoken to an old acquaintance in a while, the first thing out of their mouths is usually, "Have they found him yet?" or "Do you know where he is?" or the most ignorant question of all, "Have you talked to Jason?"

I can't help but feel they are less concerned about me than getting some scoop on my brother.

During our most recent conversation, Lance and I discussed, among other things, Jason's age progression photo on the FBI Most Wanted poster, both acknowledging it likely had little resemblance to Jason. My dad looked nearly identical to Jason in his younger years. "He has to look more like Dad when he was thin," I said, quickly scrolling through my photos to text Lance a picture of John Brown in his forties.

After seeing this new photo, Lance agreed that the age progression needed updating. He also asked me for some additional information that he felt would be helpful. I said I would dig through the boxes of Jason's belongings I'd managed to salvage from his storage space and send it over.

Even though he's on the FBI's Most Wanted list, I love my brother and there is a part of me that wants to protect him by not giving out any information that could lead to his capture and, possibly, death. Still, my conscience demands that I do the right thing and help. If Jason were to call me or contact me, I would hang up and call the FBI immediately. I have spent years programming and preparing myself for that to happen.

On September 1, 2020, I learned that Lance was retiring from the FBI. He sent me a note which said the following, "Jami, Good luck with your book and everything you do. Your willingness to do the right thing is refreshing."

Strangely, after sixteen years, I consider Lance Leising a friend. He has been the one constant and the only real connection to my brother. Although it is unlikely, I feel he is someone I can trust and talk to about Jason because he understands my pain and loss. We also have a deeper connection—we both want to find my brother, even though it is for different reasons. While I definitely consider my relationship with the FBI to be love/hate, I will certainly miss having an agent I trust on the case.

As for the always-asked question, "Where do you think Jason is?"

I honestly don't know.

For the record, I don't believe Jason is with my dad. While it would be so like both of them to just sit back and watch all this shit go down, it makes no sense. Jason did the same thing, vanishing like my dad, but for different reasons. All I can say is it's a cruel game, playing loved ones and making them worry and wonder for the rest of our lives.

I also don't believe either of them killed themselves. While my brain can and does go all sorts of places, narcissists and sociopaths don't generally kill themselves. They love themselves too much. They have a grandiose mindset that allows them to believe they are better than everyone else and will get away with whatever it is they have done.

So far, Jason has done just that and the manhunt continues to this day. Lance said they've received over 10,000 leads and still get five to six tips per week. Jason's DNA profile is on law enforcement databases around the world. They believe Jason is living in a Mormon community somewhere—possibly Salt Lake City, and I've heard there was a sighting of him in Mexico in 2017. I've heard theories about him living in Quebec, or that he went to France because he speaks fluent French. Jason doesn't do the obvious so I wouldn't be surprised if he was living in Salt Lake or Los Angeles or somewhere else in plain sight. There are so many small towns and places to blend in, meet a girl, and start a new life. In April 2020, the Mansfield News Journal reported that Jason had possibly been spotted in Richland County, Ohio.

My mind goes all over the place when I wonder where he went or where I would hide if I were on the run. I told Lance that my Dad got sloppy as he aged, as narcissists and sociopaths do. He wasn't as sharp and made mistakes. They get tired, and it takes a lot of energy to keep their lies and bullshit straight. If Jason is ever apprehended, it will be because he got sloppy and made a small mistake. Living life on the run has to wear you down at some point, so maybe he will eventually slip up. That's what the FBI is counting on.

Right after the murder, Jason apparently told Brad he wanted to "start over" and be "less materialistic." However he's done that, he's done it successfully, given he's on the FBI Ten Most Wanted Fugitives list. Of the 523 people named to the FBI's Most Wanted list since 1950, 490 have been apprehended. The list evolved as a result of a popular story in the Washington Daily News about the ten "toughest guys" the bureau wanted to arrest. Because media and outreach have always been part of the program, 162 fugitives have been located as a direct result of the help of the public. Although law enforcement believes Jason will eventually be caught, with every passing year that becomes less likely.

My dad has been missing now for over twenty-six years. Jason has been on the run for sixteen years. My older brother, Brad, hasn't spoken to me since shortly after Jason took off. My sister and I care about each other but we are very different and go for long periods of time without talking.

I spoke recently to one of my Uncle Edward's kids about genetics and how the narcissistic/sociopathic gene can be passed down like many other mental illnesses. He confirmed that a "con artist" or "street smart" tendency is prevalent throughout the family. Thankfully, Jason and my dad served as cautionary tales of what happens when whatever impulses that may exist are acted upon.

In the end, Grandfather the patriarch was leveraged to the hilt. As he and Gen started getting older, their finances came unraveled and they had nothing at the end of their lives. Bernie Brown died of heart disease on my Dad's birthday, March 4, 2000. Gen, my grandmother, died in the summer of 2005, on Brad's birthday. They both died not knowing of Jason's alleged crime. They both died alone in nursing facilities, Bernie in Pasadena, California and Gen with dementia in a nursing home in Santa Ana, California.

For years, I've known I had a story to tell. I thought I wanted people to understand who Jason was, his troubled family life, and the addictions he battled. I wanted to be Jason's voice and explain that while he'd been involved with a horrific crime, he wasn't an entirely bad person and was a product of his environment. I thought my message was that while I hated what my brother was accused of, I couldn't help but still love him as a person.

I've come to realize that the story is not that simple, nor is it just Jason's.

To be the sister, brother, or relative of one of the world's most wanted men is to live every day with the horrible truth and many of the consequences of his brutal act. My world became a lot smaller, as did my circle of friends. I am judged, for being "Jason Brown's" sister, as if somehow I am a criminal as well. People talk behind my back, and then right to my face, making me a little less trusting of who I surround myself with or share personal information with. That has changed me. The ripple effect of one person's actions affects many. It has taken me years to get to a place where I am able to accept that I am a product of the same environment as my brother, but I chose not to and wouldn't make the decisions he did. My brother, and my father before him, made very different choices. It's something I've had to learn to live with and to not have embarrass, humiliate, or define me. I have to constantly remind myself, I am not my story.

# LOST AND FOUND

Recently, I moved back near Laguna Beach, where this story all began. This time, however, I feel like I am exactly where I'm supposed to be. Instead of taking off before planting even the most shallow roots, I feel like I've come back to where my root system runs deepest.

Someone recently told me how rare it is for people who have lived through any sort of trauma to go back into that same environment later in life and help others. People I haven't seen for years will just grab my hand and tell me, "It's just mind-blowing that you've turned out this way despite everything you've been through."

While my brother may have committed an inexcusable act of violence and his disappearance continues to be a subject of interest and speculation, we both grew up Brown together. Jason and I were taught to run. He is, literally, on the run, while I have spent my entire life on the move—changing things up as I go, and not away from but toward my next adventure or learning experience.

Now that I have stopped running, there have been times where the silence has been so deafening I can hear my heartbeat. I still suffer from extreme insomnia because the nights remain the hardest part. When the world is quiet, I am left with only my thoughts and myself and it's challenging to turn off my brain.

I used to think that I would be happy and fulfilled by certain milestones—at thirty, or when a particular thing happened, or when I found that perfect guy. After spending a lifetime in and out of relationships with men, making them my primary focus, I am learning to be alone and working to develop a relationship with myself. I have learned that I have enough and I am enough. I can do it on my own. I don't need someone else to validate who I am. I don't need someone else to do something for me or think if I do this for them, are they going to love me or are they going to be there for me. I don't do it anymore. I tell people no, and I don't feel any guilt.

As my son Logan, who is in many ways a teacher to me, said, "Mom, stop worrying and caring for everyone else, just do you. Just do Jami."

I love the saying, *The lesson is not having pain void from your life, it is the struggle. It is the overcoming.*

As sad as it is, often it is only through our most painful experiences that we learn the most about our inner strength and what we are made of. My mess is my message. These are the lessons that made me tough and the new problems I face seem minimal in comparison. Now, I get up every day and face challenges asking myself, *What is the lesson?*

I know only I have the power to decide how I am going to react.

I learned the hard way that life is a process—a process of learning, evolving, changing, and growing. I am still learning every day. I am also making mistakes, but I'm not so hard on myself anymore. I don't self-sabotage. I don't compare myself to others. I chose to look forward, and not back. When I find that I am veering off my path I adjust my sails and pull myself back on course. I accept my life as mine. I am grateful for the lessons, opportunities, and challenges. It has shaped me into who I am today— a wise, caring compassionate soul. I keep my heart and mind wide open, but I am more careful who surround myself with. I always wanted a big family, but that never happened. Instead, I've been blessed to be able to choose my friends and the people I call family and I am surrounded by them. Family is about trust, love and connection, and not necessarily the family into which we are born.

I have learned that you have to find a purpose in life, bigger than yourself, serving and helping others is a special gift I have, and that is where I find true joy and purpose. It is my path.

A spiritual guide asked me recently, "Do you love, Jami? Do you have love in your heart?

I answered, "Absolutely. Yes."

"Then that is all that matters," she said. "Love wins."

I try and hold that in my heart as I face my all that life throws my way from here on out.

# ACKNOWLEDGMENTS

When I set out to write this book, I thought it was because I needed to share a difficult story about my missing father and brother and the experiences that led up to these tragedies. I didn't expect the story to become as much about my journey as a sister and a daughter learning to survive in the midst of it all. I also didn't expect the outpouring of true love and support from the various people you have met in these pages. Whether you know their real names or not, their presence in my life has been invaluable in more ways than they'll ever know. To those of you who have remained constants, as well as those who have reentered during the process of writing this book, you have taught me so much about who I am, where I come from, and who in this world is the most important to me. To my lifelong friends, family and "other" mothers and dads—you know who you are—thank you for the love and support. And to you, the readers, thank you! I am truly grateful to all of you for taking the time to learn about me and the story of my past as I head forward on my path.

# SOURCES

While CENTER OF ATTENTION is primarily recounted from my life experiences and the recollections of family and friends, I confirmed the accuracy of the details surrounding my father's disappearance, the Ahwatukee AMC 24 robbery and murder, and my brother's involvement by consulting a number of sources. They include the FBI, the Orange County Sheriff's office, as well as the following:

"AG—112 Jason Derek Brown." *American Greed*. Season 10, Kurtis Productions, 14 Jul. 2016.

"The Fugitive Jason Derek Brown." *Dateline*. NBC News, 24 Mar. 2013.

Williams, Paige. *The Ghost*. Byliner Inc. 2012. E book.

Boyle, Louise. "FBI's Most Wanted fugitive 'could be hiding among Mormon community' after EIGHT YEARS on the run." dailymail. co.uk. Daily Mail.com, 26 Nov.2012. Web. 16 Nov 2020.

Marcinko, Tom. "Arizona's Most Wanted." phoenixmag.com. Phoenix Magazine, 1, Mar. 2014. Web. 16 Nov.2020.

McFall, Michael. "FBI: most wanted fugitive hiding among Mormons?" sltrib.com. The Salt Lake Tribune, 27 Nov. 2012. Web. 16 Nov. 2020.

Newcomb, Alyssa. "Most Wanted Fugitive Jason Brown Could Be Hiding Among Mormons." ABCnews.go.com. ABC News, 26 Nov. 2012. Web.16 Nov.2020.

Williams, Paige. "What Happened to a Mormon Missionary Turned America's Most Wanted?" thedailybeast.com. The Daily Beast, 13 Jul. 2017. Web. 16 Nov.2020.

"FBI Ten Most Wanted Fugitives by year, 1950," Wikipedia:The Free Encyclopedia, Wikimedia Foundation, Inc., 31 Dec. 2019. Web. Nov. 2020, https://en.wikipedia.org/wiki/FBI_Ten_Most_Wanted_Fugitives_by_year,_1950.

"Jason Derek Brown," Wikipedia: The Free Encyclopedia, Wikimedia Foundation Inc., 25 Oct 2020. Web 16 Nov.2020, https://en.wikipedia.org/wiki/Jason_Derek_Brown.

There are many, many more articles about my brother. New ones—mainly concerning sightings and conjecture as to his possible whereabouts—are added regularly.

CPSIA information can be obtained
at www.ICGtesting.com
Printed in the USA
LVHW041922230421
685378LV00027B/604/J

9 781736 290705